Everyday Humanism

Everyday Humanism

Edited by

Dale McGowan and Anthony B. Pinn

SHEFFIELD UK   BRISTOL CT

Published by Equinox Publishing Ltd.

UK: Office 415, The Workstation, 15 Paternoster Row, Sheffield S1 2BX
USA: ISD, 70 Enterprise Drive, Bristol, CT 06010

www.equinoxpub.com

First published 2014

ISBN-13 978 1 78179 044 1   (hardback)
              978 1 78179 045 8   (paperback)

British Library Cataloguing-in-Publication Data

A catalogue record for this book is available from the British Library.

Library of Congress Cataloging-in-Publication Data

Library of Congress Cataloging-in-Publication Data

Everyday humanism / edited by Dale McGowan and Anthony B. Pinn.
     pages cm
 Includes bibliographical references and index.
 ISBN 978-1-78179-044-1 (hb) -- ISBN 978-1-78179-045-8 (pb)
 1. Humanism. I. McGowan, Dale, editor.
 B821.E94 2014
 144--dc23
                                    2014011980

Typeset by ISB Typesetting, Sheffield, UK

Printed and bound by Lightning Source Inc. (La Vergne, TN), Lighting Source UK Ltd. (Milton Keynes), Lightning Source AU Pty. (Scoresby, Victoria)

Contents

Acknowledgements

Dale McGowan and Anthony B. Pinn

We want to express our thanks to several people. First of all to Janet Joyce and Valerie Hall of Equinox Publishing for their encouragement and patience. From the start they saw the value of this project, and we are grateful for that. In addition, we want to express our gratitude to the contributors to this volume, and our thanks to the Board of the Institute for Humanist Studies for its support. We would also like to thank Audrey Mann and Iain Beswick for their work in editing and typesetting the manuscript on behalf of Equinox. Finally, we must also thank Jason Jeffries – one of Pinn's graduate students – for constructing the bibliography, and Darrius Hills for preparing the index to this volume.

Introduction

Dale McGowan and Anthony B. Pinn

This book is not an apology for humanism; it isn't an effort to justify the presence of humanism, nor to argue for its place in our collective social life. Instead, we assume the importance of humanism as a particular life orientation for a growing group across the globe. Drawing on that assumption, we offer approaches to thinking about being a humanist in the world, approaching the nature and meaning of relationships in the world, and finally reflection on approaches to doing humanism, or put differently, humanist ways of acting in light of the mundane demands of life. In that way, the chapters in this book promote the value of humanism at the level of the ordinary, typical occurrences and conditions of our existence.

Various organizations and individuals over the past decade have worked hard to present to the public an apology for humanism, one that points out its strengths and potential contributions to public debate and public arrangements of life. Compared to theistic orientations, it has been argued, humanism's attention to reason and human history makes for a better philosophy of life and promotes a grounded sense of both humanity's shortcomings and potentials. This apology for humanism has argued, for example, that one does not need God or gods in order to live productive and responsible lives. Materials related to this take on humanism have been important and much needed to the extent they offer a macro-ethics. In other words they offer valuable, general guidelines that tackle the more public (often abstract) configuration of our collective existence.

What is needed at this point is more attention to the manner in which humanism – as a life philosophy and orientation – impacts and informs the everyday concerns that shape our living. How might humanist principles impact parenting? How might these principles inform our take on aging, on health, on death, on friendship, on relationships, on giving? These are just a few of the issues around everyday life that need interpretation from a humanist perspective. In response, this volume seeks to move the discussion of humanism's positive contributions to life away from the macro-level to attention to the everyday, or micro, dimensions of our individual and collective existence. In a word, it works to present the *human* in humanism.

To serve the book's intent to provide snapshots of how humanists have (or at least might) view and respond to the challenges and opportunities of mundane life, the tone of the chapters is conversational. While we have worked to control academic jargon, some of the pieces offer more personal reflection than others, and this is a natural consequence of the demands posed by particular topics. Some call for more personal context than others. Nonetheless, all are based not on a strictly objective view of the entanglements of human life, but rather they are subjective, and interested, charged by a shared commitment to humanism as a productive life path and strategy.

Facets of Humanist Life

Three areas – being a humanist, humanists in relationship, and doing humanism – constitute the three sections of the volume. In the first, contributors explore dimensions of how humanists encounter the world.

Jennifer Michael Hecht probes the meaning and the value of life in a world not controlled and orchestrated by divine forces. Hecht begins a conversation regarding how humanists might think about the challenges of, as she puts it, living "in a meaning rupture because we are human and the universe is not." In conversation with French Existentialists and others, Hecht reflects on what humanism offers humanists living in light of a desire for justice and meaning in a world marked by realities that push against that desire. In short, as Hecht argues, "life matters," and it has meaning, while "the feeling of meaning is sufficient to the definition of meaning." So, we press on through life, working to improve circumstances because it is what we can do. She ties this discussion to the issue of suicide and argues while theists can deny, or push aside with a cosmic broom, realities difficult to process, humanists cannot. And while humanism has traditionally embraced the right to end life – to commit suicide – Hecht argues that we "feel life" and "if we want to feel it more of the time, we have to work on it" as we do, for instance, with love relationships. In short, humanists live in a challenging world, but one that isn't devoid of hope, love, and the stuff that makes life as meaningful as our human skills and strength will allow.

With this perspective on the world and our place in the world outlines, the second chapter by Dale McGowan tackles fear, with a particular concern for how humanist parents might address issues of fear with children. Using stories to tease out what fear is meant to produce in children – safety, alertness, longevity – McGowan tackles the negative dimensions of fear. He suggests fear has resulted in the survival of human life as potential dangers and traumas are avoided, but the benefits have for the most part hit their expiration date. That is, "In a world of 7 billion people in close quarters, it's no longer quite so adaptive to have everybody all edgy and shooty all the time." Here's the problem: "Our brains don't know that." The sad outcome is this: In our time, fear doesn't necessarily have a direct correspondence to actual danger, and fear is often misplaced causing us to actually fail to recognize real threats. Religious conservatism, according to McGowan, plays into this fear problem. The best approach to this situation is to reduce inherited fear, and teach children to recognize and address fear in ways that inspire "confidence and security."

McGowan's chapter speaks to religious conservatism and its connection to unhealthy fear, but he also notes a distinction between the need for religion (as a response to and safeguarding of unhealthy fear) and religion embraced for other reasons. This raises the question of how humanists should interact with theists. In a word, what are the possibilities for cooperation between nontheists and theists? This question is taken up in the final essay of the first section, in which Chris Stedman points out not only the ability of nontheists to collaborate and cooperate with theists, but the very need for such alliances. Neither theisms nor nontheist orientations are going away; people will continue to embrace each. Hence, what Stedman suggests is a posture marked by appreciation for diversity of opinion, but appreciation that grows out of each party being "grounded in her or his own particular story and identity." Why is this important? Stedman offers five reasons: nontheists are outnumbered and are not in a position to advance an agenda of justice without assistance; ending religious extremism requires more moderate groups to work based on shared values – for example, rejection of extremism and promotion of productive alliances – as opposed to a preoccupation with difference; there is much nontheists need to learn about others and this requires open lines of communication and a willingness to recognize "mutual interests" that can improve the impact of activism; the manner in which nontheists face discrimination demands the forging of allies and the effort to "make themselves known" in order to improve their image; and lastly, after all, "engagement and compassion" are core values for humanists and it only makes sense to apply this value to encounters with theists.

The second section begins with Greg Epstein's discussion of community within a humanist context. Building on his work at Harvard University as well as insights drawn from developments elsewhere, Epstein argues for solid attention to the need of humanists for connection to others, for ways, locations, and times to celebrate, mourn, and work for the betterment of the world. In this way, Epstein points beyond understanding of humanism that involve simple negation: what humanists critique and what humanists don't believe, to what humanism affirms, practices, and advances.

Following Epstein's chapter, the volume offers a guide for those seeking resources for educating children consistent with humanist principles and values. Bob Bhaerman moves readers through an annotated bibliography of books, websites, and organizations that provide useful materials for parents and others interested in educating vis-à-vis humanism as a method of critical thinking. The idea, according to Bhaerman, isn't indoctrination but rather "inoculation" against poor reasoning and against a failure to use critical thinking skills. (Critical thinking is a phrase and method Bob references over and over again in this chapter.) Nurturing future generations in ways that will equip them to address various forms of oppression requires synergy between "education, action, and community building." Achieving this synergy involves attention to several obligations revolving around advancement of essential skills, the teaching of science, and the promotion of humanist education based on critical thinking, and so on, within local, national and international environments. Bhaerman argues that the pedagogy should be grounded in a set of moral codes including altruism, empathy, global awareness and humility.

In the next chapter, Anne Klaeysen uses personal narrative to frame a discussion of rituals and celebrate relationships. As Klaeysen notes at the beginning of her piece, "Contrary to popular perceptions, humanism maintains a deep regard for the emotionally-charged connections between individuals and groups. It has an abiding interest in and response to the nature of human life meaning revolving around practices of love." The challenge, then, is fostering ways to formally recognize and celebrate these connections. Klaeysen offers several examples of how humanists might ritualize their celebration of love – weddings, baby namings, and memorial services. Each example, complete with an "order of service," so to speak, is meant to offer a way to think about the importance of expressing connection but also to recognize the deeply human (and humanistic) drive to do so.

Maintaining a similar approach of personal narrative from which more general ideas are drawn, Susan Rose's essay begins where Klaeysen's ends, with the loss of love through death: the memorial service. The humanist understanding that there is nothing beyond this life, that we are bound in and by human history, encourages understanding of the memorial service as an opportunity to, "stop and pay attention to a change in our lives," while recognizing we have a new and different relationship to the deceased. That is to say, "We don't know what happens after we die, so we must give our attention to living the life we know as best we can."

The third section of the book begins with attention to humanism and political life. Andrew Copson argues humanists must give attention to politics but not politics limited to a sense of necessity – politics as the demand of social animals for "effective communal living" to a sense of politics as virtue – "the admirable craft by which we build a better world." The former – the demand for effective communal living – might be the origins of politics, but humanists, Copson urges, must recognize virtue as the current and pressing approach to politics and political life. This is not to deny the need for survival promoted by this first form of politics, but humanists should recognize what we envision as the "good" society (a democratic and secular society) is a human endeavor neatly fit within the realm of politics. Humanist fulfillment as a societal aim and a political task includes attention to freedom, equality, and fulfillment – that is, personal development. In a word, "The rule of law, democracy and human rights, underpinned as they are by the equality of every person in the face of justice, the equal right of every person to a say in the decision-making processes, and the aspiration of a minimum standard of treatment that every person can be guaranteed, seem to be the essential building blocks of a political order a humanist could support."

Chapter 9, written by Henk Manschot and Caroline Šuranský, maintains a political theme, but this time the focus involves humanism and ecological issues. They propose the "current ecological crisis is foremost a crisis of values" as opposed to involving conditions that can be correct through "economic, political, and technological changes" alone. By this they mean it has to do with worldviews and with the significance placed on particular arrangements and processes for living. Turning attention to correctives, Manschot and Suransky argue humanism, although seldom applied to ecological issues, is a particular worldview that holds great promise for addressing ecological destruction, by both offering critical information concerning the basis for the crisis and by encouraging an alternate set of values through which to positively alter the current circumstances. This entails movement from a human-centered worldview, which is the common framing, to a life-centered worldview. The latter entails recognizing humanity is a late development and that the wellbeing of the world involves more than the health of humanity, in fact it might entail more limited concern to our own wants and desires, and more attention to the needs of a larger system of life. Ultimately, getting to this point requires knowledge, passion, and action.

The next chapter draws on a similar concern with proper ethical conduct. However, it does so through attention to charity. Anthony Pinn argues charity often entails a subtext that is problematic: giving is really about the giver as opposed to the one receiving assistance. In addition, charity often covers and distracts from much needed attention to deconstruction of the fundamental sources of inequality and injustice – racism, sexism, classism and so on. Drawing from figures such as Henry David Thoreau and Albert Camus, Pinn urges humanists to make use of an alternate orientation toward the "other." This involves recognition that systemic issues must be addressed and, without this, "giving" has limited sustained and felt impact. Connected to this is a different posture toward our activism, one through which we recognize difficulties will persist despite our efforts, but that we work to make changes because it is what we can do. Such thinking flies in the face of theism's assurances based on the work of god(s), and it corrects for the hyper optimism that often influences humanism. And, it does this without collapsing into nihilism. What we have, through this reorientation, are practices of shared existence that are not properly called charity but rather simply constitute living in ways that promote life.

The final chapter turns readers back to the issue of the end of life, and it does so through attention – from a humanist perspective – on advance care directives. Unlike some of the chapters, Katrina Scott's thoughts do not explicitly name humanism nor humanists, but rather her insights and suggestions are guided by an underpinning of humanist sensibilities. Like Klaeysen, Rose, and several others in this volume, Scott frames her chapter with personal experience, a personal narrative that highlights key concerns and possibilities applicable to humanists (and nonhumanists) alike. After outlining various scenarios and considerations based on the nature of medicine and healthcare, Scott makes her perspective clear: be proactive, act now. That is to say, talk with family and friends because "the more your wishes concerning end of life care, the better chance you have at having someone listen."

Its Purpose

In this book we attempt to cover a variety of everyday developments, experiences, and needs – and we do so in a way that centers humanism as a vital life orientation with the capacity to inform the "good" life. And, through the inclusion of US and European scholars and activists, we have worked to offer this information in ways that include but extend beyond the United States. This international perspective is vital if presentation of humanist life is to reflect the rich geography of humanism's presence.

It is our hope the suggestions, insights, and cautions presented here will point out the wealth of opportunity for living well and living in relationship lodged in nontheistic orientations. That is to say, humanism does more than promote a platform for challenging the separation of church and state or the advocating of science education. While important, these areas of concern and activism don't capture necessarily all the nuance and details of our private lives; and, it is life from the private to the public that we seek to capture in these pages. Put differently, there is something about the dynamics of our private lives that inform our public stance.

We believe this volume is important for humanists in that it provides as sense of the human in humanism; it promotes a sense of the shared ordinary challenges and struggles, opportunities and moments of celebration that inform human life – even when that human life is without any attention to god(s). Yet, all of this, all the stuff of ordinary life impacts us whether one claims to be a humanist or not; and so, we offer it to nonhumanists as well as a way to reflect upon the activities of the human embedded in *human*ity.

Section I:

On Being a Humanist

1   On the Meaning of Life

Jennifer Michael Hecht*

We live in a meaning rupture because we are human and the universe is not. Religion can be seen as a "world-fixing" attempt to reconcile our most irreconcilable experiences. Religion is, however, only one way of dealing with the paradox of being human in a nonhuman world. Those of us who value reality above tradition find explanations and comforts elsewhere. For most of us, to live a rich human life we need to address our cosmic situation in some way. This chapter considers the human predicament and zeroes in on a few ways that philosophy and art can help.

The differences between the human and the universe are many but here are a few of the real standout issues. Human beings seem to have a native sense of justice. The universe seems to reward and punish the kind and the cruel in equal measure. Human beings are full of desires. The universe rolls along without the thrust of desire. We see our lives in stories, with a beginning, middle, and an end. The universe runs us through a random life, and then ends it, with no sense of balanced narrative. We are fixated on the idea that great effort leads to success, but in this world some people can sing and

---

*   Jennifer Michael Hecht earned a PhD in the history of science from Columbia University. Her collections of poetry include the highly praised *The Next Ancient World* (2001)—which won the Tupelo Press Judge's Prize in Poetry, the Poetry Society of America's Norma Farber First Book Award, and *ForeWord Review*'s Poetry Book of the Year Award—and *Funny* (2005), winner of the Felix Pollak Prize in Poetry. Known for her wit and erudition, Hecht's poetry frequently draws on her work as an intellectual historian. *The Next Ancient World* mixes contemporary and ancient worldviews, histories, myths, and ideas, and *Funny* explores the implications of the human love of humor and jokes. Hecht's prose has also been widely praised for the breadth of its scholarship. Her books include *Doubt: A History* (2003); *The End of the Soul: Scientific Modernity, Atheism, and Anthropology in France* (2003), which won the prestigious Ralph Waldo Emerson Award from the Phi Beta Kappa Society; and *The Happiness Myth: The Historical Antidote to What Isn't Working Today* (2008).

some cannot, some people get lucky and some have to learn to cope without what we ache for. We imbue everything with meaning. The universe offers us no reason for its being.

Our sense of time and space is also peculiar to humanity. We usually give our attention to things that happen within a human life span, a few generations, or at most in the span of written history. Outside the human mind, time is vast: The universe is 13 billion years old; the dinosaurs were on earth for 165 million years; humans have been around for 200,000 years; and written history goes back about 6,000 years. On the contrary, mice live their full lives in one to three years; houseflies and bees live four weeks; some mayfly species live a whole life span in half an hour. As for space: we normally give our attention to things that exist on the scale of human senses, especially things that are a size we can see with unaided eyes. The universe has hundreds of billions of galaxies, which typically have hundreds of billions of stars; our sun could fit in the largest star we know of 165,000 times; earth could fit in our sun about 1,300,000 times; and on our tiny planet, there are seven billion people. On the other end of the spectrum, a human body is made up of about a hundred trillion atoms. Almost all our worries and hopes, plans and fears, grief and joy, take place on this infinitesimally particular point of interest on a mind-boggling continuum of time and space.

We persist in our human perceptions and concerns despite all this evidence that the universe does not support them.

Religion attempts to remedy this meaning rupture in one of two ways. Religions either impose humanness on the universe, imagining the heavens' mind, purpose, plans, and justice; and seeing this superhuman intelligence as valuing the human scale. Or we try to impose the inhumanness of the universe on ourselves, training ego out of our personalities, meditating on the vast expanses of time and space, learning to take ourselves less seriously.

Many religions do a bit of each. For instance, on the one hand most sects of the Christian religion see God as world-fixing and as a personality, giving answers to the unfathomable questions of the universe by God's very authority. Also, we can ask this Christian God to fulfill our longings. More things, more love, more attention. On the other hand, Jesus exhorts his followers to give everything away, leave one's family, stop one's cravings. Consider Buddhism. Theravada Buddhism holds that there is no God and we are each responsible for training ourselves to a state of mind that has much in common with the nonhuman universe. Mahayana Buddhism imagines the world as corrected by karma, by rewards in the next life, by ornate fantastical images of an unseen world. Judaism generally sees God as a solution to the problems of death, meaning in life, consolation, and guidance; but, as with other religions, it has a long history of a mystical side where adherents starve themselves, take vows of silence, meditate on numbers and phrases, and struggle to suppress their normal human ego, lust, hunger, love, and conversation. Very often these practices are purposefully taken on to help a participant have a trance-like experience of being one with the universe, outside the usual human predicament.

Human beings do not need to correct the world through our imaginations, but we do need to give the problem some thought. The concept of justice is an ideal place to begin. In Western religion, varied though it is, it is generally agreed that there is a providential God who weighs our behavior and makes up for worldly unfairness with an eternity of either joy or torture. Judaism does not speak of hell, but still envisions an afterlife that is a dyad of those who go to heaven and those who are left out.

Yet even the Bible doesn't ignore the fact that the world does not conform to the human sense of justice. As we are told in Ecclesiastes (9:11), "The race is not to the swift, nor the battle to the strong, neither yet bread to the wise, nor yet riches to men of understanding, nor yet favor to men of skill; but time and chance happeneth to them all." Scholars estimate this book of the Bible as having been written at the end of the third century BCE. By this time Judaism has begun to develop a notion of the afterlife, but Ecclesiastes argues against the idea of an afterlife, so there is no thought of justice arriving after death either.

The afterlife is not imagined in all cultures (and in many which have some kind of afterlife it is only for a tiny fraction of the population), but tensions around the idea of justice are pervasive across cultures. World over, humans seem to come into consciousness, as children, with an innate sense of fairness. We can see that the world is not fair, but we are outraged by its unfairness. We plead with parents and other authorities to make things fair. We dream of revenge or take recompense against unfairness. Yet the animal world around us is brutally unfair, and the physical world of the universe doesn't show any signs of knowing the meaning of justice. Some generous, loving, creative, wise people get sick and die young, while some selfish, abusive, sneering, talentless, fools live long and prosperous lives.

God and gods are an imagined mind of the universe and they have the attributes of fairness we wish the universe had. The Greek gods were not concerned with fairness for everyone at all times, but they judged outrageous bad behavior and remarkable good behavior and punished or rewarded people in response. The one God of the Jewish, Christian, and Muslim traditions is often described as doing things that do not seem at all fair (did no one in the town of Gomorrah deserve to live?),[1] but as we have

1.   Genesis 19.

received his general description in modern times, he is said to be the keeper of justice, and dedicated to meting out appropriate rewards for everyone, in this life or in a world after death.

In our present-day culture the idea of a single world-fixing God is so pervasive that it is hard to think about justice without either believing in this God or actively not believing in this God. Many human groups never had a concept of a God. They found other ways of coping with the meaning rupture. Human beings need something to help them have a rich and good life. Our capacity for thought, evaluation, imagination, and desire is too powerful to exist without community and culture. Without some version of community and culture we lose our minds. Indeed, our sanity cannot be described in the absence of community and culture. We need something from each other, but we do not need God.

It does not always feel that way if you recently believed in God, or even if you just live in a culture that includes the notion of such a God. Consider a bit of an extended metaphor: In a cold and desolate world, a man with a bearskin coat will love his bearskin coat and if you take it away to give him lightweight microfiber down, there will be a moment in which he is freezing and scared, and then a long time when he is warm and almost weightless, but he misses his bearskin coat like an old friend. Even if you take him into a land of sunshine and light, he may miss the old coat as a naked turtle would miss his shell.

Yet when a man has never owned a bearskin coat, he will be happy with microfiber down in winter and tee shirts in summer. He will see a bearskin coat hanging in a museum and it will look as heavy as a bear, and aromatically ursine as well.

The idea of God has been the bear coat for many, but most people through history have used other methods to warm themselves. Billions of Confucians have lived and died in a system of this-world meaning, which honors those who have come before, and defines a code of respect and duty, but has no inherent supernaturalism or God. Millions of people have lived with the guidance of Buddhism, which has two main branches: the Theravada, who believe in no God, gods, or supernaturalism; and the Mahayana, who believe in a fanciful universe where karma dictates reincarnation, and magical "Buddaverses" await the most enlightened. The Mahanyana are surely not what we think of as rationalist, but note that they do very well indeed without any notion of a Western God – an invisible singular being in the sky who made us, and watches us, judges us, listens to our prayers and petitions, and will be there, to punish or comfort, when we die.

It is also true that millions of people who do or did believe in God did not believe in a God anything like the average modern-day depiction of him.

Aristotle suggested that the universe might have a Prime Mover, something that gave energy to the world, but he did not believe this source of power made human beings, or provides a life after death, or is a source of meaning, or even knows that we are here. The medieval theologian and philosopher Moses Maimonides, one of the greatest Jewish sages of all time, wrote of "negative theology" in which one only describes God in terms of what he is not, so that we never forget that this notion of God refers to something entirely unknowable. Maimonides wrote that we cannot even say that God exists.

Today many sophisticated religious people do not believe in petitionary prayer and indeed think of prayer more as a ritual for human pleasure than as an actual communication with a listening God. Many people who believe in God will not assert a single attribute for this name: not that he is a "being," not that he made us, not that there is life after death, not that there is justice. For some, God is love, and while they know that using the word "God" adds nothing to their view of the universe, they still enjoy thinking of themselves as believers.

Nevertheless, in modern America, the word "God" brings to mind certain attributes. We think of Michelangelo's God on the ceiling of the Sistine Chapel: bearded, robed, fatherly. We think of the triad of ultimate qualities: omniscient, omnipotent, eternal. Many Christians think of Jesus instead, a younger, gentler figure, but also all knowing, all powerful, and everlasting. These visions of God generally entail the world-correcting ideas that we have already mentioned: meaning in life, effective prayer, and life after death.

People who have grown up with this idea of God and later come to a naturalist worldview will often have some longing for their former belief. Some will experience their new condition with a sense of grief. It should be noted that many people leave religion partly because they were abused in the name of God, and while some of these people may grieve the loss of religious "answers," such people are also likely to celebrate the freedom from an oppressive doctrine. If the people who tell you about God are not kind, nothing could be more frightening and disturbing as the idea of an all-knowing, all-seeing, all-powerful God who can punish you for eternity.

Even if you never believed, if you grew up in a culture that included this idea of God, you may find yourself wishing you believed. This modern idea of God seems to take care of so many needs. We were all children once and we remember what it was like to have someone to whom we could report our needs, someone to plead for things we want, someone to thank for our good fortune, someone to be angry at when life is unfair, and someone we could trust to redress our insults. Likewise, not everyone fears death, but many people do. Of course many people who believe in God still fear death, but nonbelievers sometimes fantasize about a belief so strong that it eradicates fear of death. Believers are also to be found lamenting the meaninglessness of life, and nonbelievers sometimes dream of a God who removes the problem of meaning.

As I have suggested above, many people who believe in God are still plagued with these problems. Some are not convinced they believe in the kind of God who is that concerned with individuals. Some do essentially believe in that God, but still have to work very hard to keep this belief in the forefront of their minds. The most common prayer one sees in literature is, essentially, "Lord help me in my disbelief."

Because of all these cultural complications, it can be difficult to think about the idea of meaning on its own terms. If we are going to think about the meaning of life, we have to first get a little distance from the idea of God. If we can remember that millions of people have lived without that idea, we can see that the idea of the meaning as dependent on God disappears.

One of the central reasons that atheism today is associated with meaninglessness is Existentialism. In the middle of the last century, the French philosopher Jean-Paul Sartre claimed that "existence precedes essence," meaning that human beings are entirely what they make of themselves. Each human being is completely responsible for any sense of human meaning he or she may have: "Man first of all exists, encounters himself, surges up in the world – and defines himself afterwards. If man as the existentialist sees him is not definable, it is because to begin with he is nothing."[2] For Sartre, a human being is only "what he makes of himself." And why? – Because of the absence of God. "[T]here is no human nature, because there is no God to have a conception of it."[3]

Sartre thinks that because there is no God, there is no human meaning outside the idea of him. Yet we have abundant evidence that life was meaningful to millions of people who lived without the idea of God.

What Sartre calls his "Atheistic Existentialism," is, to my mind, a withdrawal symptom. If you were recently an addict, you experience a day without drugs very differently than people who are not addicts. You miss something you had become deeply used to, and the world now seems harsh and empty without it. So it is with belief in God.

Through history the essentially unanimous conclusion of great minds of secularism has been that essence precedes existence. That is, being human already means a great deal before we start making personal decisions. Human culture is a world of meaning.

---

2.   Jean Paul Sartre, "Existentialism is a Humanism," in Walter Kaufman, ed., *Existentialism from Dostoyevsky to Sartre* (New York: Meridian, 1989).

3.   Sartre, "Existentialism is a Humanism," p. 349.

If you wanted to learn about an elephant, or a meerkat, or an ant, it would not be sufficient to take one animal into a laboratory and have a look at it. Nor can you understand yourself in isolation. Humans living together make meaning in their relationships. This would be so even if you randomly chose ten people from around the globe who shared neither language nor history nor ethnicity and put them in a house for a while. For most people, of course, shared culture adds immeasurably to this natural meaning.

As I have been defining it for many years now: *The feeling of meaning is sufficient to the definition of meaning.* Just as love exists though it is not a material thing that can be reduced to measurement, so meaning exists. We would not, normally, lay down our own life, nor the lives of those we love, nor even take the lives of anonymous strangers. We feel that life matters. We do not need this mattering to be caused by some other being.

Indeed, what exactly would a God bring to this problem? If an awesome being showed up and declared himself God, and wowed us with some astounding displays, we might still find ourselves with some unsolvable problems. What could this God say to reconcile us to the outrageous, unthinkable suffering of so many children, women, and men (in slavery, in massacre, in degradation); of billions of abused and slaughtered animals; or even of privileged people in their nightmares, grief, and private battles? Could the spectacle of a being called "God" reconcile us to such horrors?

It seems we are better off with a definition of justice and meaning that takes this world on its own terms. There are many ways of doing this, most of which continue to strive for justice and meaning but accept these projects as human and may or may not see the goal as ultimately possible. For those of us who find it hard to sustain such earnest hope, it is good to make use of the concept of the Absurd. It originates with the philosophy of Soren Kierkegaard in the nineteenth century, but is most powerfully advanced by the twentieth-century French philosopher Albert Camus. Kierkegaard's belief system was complicated, but Camus tried to understand our world without correcting it with a God or any other supernaturalism. Instead, Camus invited us to see the human experience of the world as absurd and to accept it as such. He understood anguish and keen frustration, but he wrote that our absurd life is worth living. Camus fought mightily for moral justice. He risked death by joining the French Resistance in World War II, he later struggled for passivism and for human rights in several guises, including a powerful crusade to end to the death penalty. He also counselled fiercely against suicide.[4]

4.   See for example Camus, *The Myth of Sisyphus and Other Essays* (New York: Vintage International, 1991); Camus, *The Rebel* (New York: Vintage International, 1991).

Philosophical thought can give us support in classic moral struggles, and can help us to press forward into new territory.

Consider one issue of life and death. In my new book, *Stay: A History of Suicide and the Philosophies against It* (New Haven: Yale University Press, 2013), I argue that suicide is wrong. This is an unusual position for a modern atheist. In the culture wars of the western world, the anti-suicide position is usually taken up by the religious, while secularists argue that without God to say it is wrong, suicide is a morally neutral act, and we all have the right to do it if we choose.

I certainly do not believe that there is a God who has forbidden suicide, or anything for that matter. Yet, like Sartre's hangover, I think that arguing in favor of despair suicide only makes sense in opposition to God. When we take the question on its own terms things look very different indeed.

I am not at all against what I call "end of life management," which is often called "assisted suicide." If a person has a painful fatal disease, like advanced cancer, physician assisted suicide is really just managing how the cancer kills you. It is an arbitrary notion, but I might suggest that if you have three friends, two relatives, and one doctor who all think it is appropriate for you to end your life, you should be able to do so. That need not be the only possible criteria, but it might be a serviceable one to contemplate.

Despair suicide is something else again. For one thing, many despair suicides speak or write of themselves as burdens to those they love; yet, their suicide would be a much greater burden. In fact, one suicide very often leads to more suicides. Studies in sociology, epidemiology, and psychology show that one suicide in a community leads to more suicides. It has been shown to be true in high schools, colleges, army battalions, reservations, particular professions, families, and even among strangers related only by age and gender. Suicide is also homicide: you take somebody with you. A 2010 study from John's Hopkins University in the May 2010 issue of *The Journal of the American Academy of Child and Adolescent Psychiatry* showed that children (18 years old or younger) of suicide victims are three times as likely to commit suicide at some future point, as compared with people who pass those ages with parents still alive.[5] As I demonstrate in *Stay*, hundreds of studies have shown this effect to be robust across many varied relationships

5.   "Children Who Lose a Parent to Suicide More Likely to Die the Same Way, Study Finds," *Science Daily*, April 21, 2010. Holly C. Wilcox, Satoko J. Kuramoto, Paul Lichtenstein, Niklas Långström, David A. Brent and Bo Runeson, "Psychiatric Morbidity, Violent Crime, and Suicide among Children and Adolescents Exposed to Parental Death." *Journal of the American Academy of Child & Adolescent Psychiatry*, May 2010.

– even people who do not know the victim but feel kinship with her or him in terms of even such broad aspects as age and gender.

Not only does the suicide harm the community, by robbing the world of yourself, and by modeling death as a response to misery, you also do an injustice to your future self. No one is an entirely integrated personality. All sorts of studies and reports show us that the vast majority of suicidal people are not suicidal all day, every day, for years on end. Rather, suicide appears to be strikingly impulse oriented. It is not right to let one bad mood murder all your other moods.

I am not alone in making these associations and coming to these conclusions. The early-twentieth-century Austrian philosopher Ludwig Wittgenstein wrote that "If anything is forbidden, suicide is forbidden; and if suicide is not forbidden, nothing is forbidden."[6] He knew what he was talking about: Wittgenstein struggled with depression and suicidal ideation throughout his life. Shockingly, three of his four brothers killed themselves, as did a cousin. Ludwig did not, and it seems he made this choice because he had read Arthur Schopenhauer's argument against suicide, and because he had thought it through himself and decided it was wrong.

What could Wittgenstein have meant in saying that "if anything is forbidden, suicide is"? He added that suicide was like a test case of the meaning of morality, just as one could study mercury vapor as a way to study all vapors. Morally wrong actions are not morally wrong simply because they harm someone else, such that anything you do to yourself is morally neutral. Instead, the human project is an endeavor of defending meaning against the abyss, defending the human against the cold, hard, unfeeling universe. Thus the ultimate crime, the crime that defines all others, is rejecting life, refusing to do even the first thing to help believe community and humanity into being.

The ancient world's most important suicide was that of Socrates, and in that prison room where he would soon calmly imbibe the hemlock that he'd been ordered to take, Socrates told his friends and students that suicide was wrong (unless, like him, one was compelled to do it by the state). For his part, Plato wrote that suicide was wrong because we must have the courage "stay at our posts" as a guard stays at his post. Aristotle wrote that suicide is wrong because it is cruel to the community to remove yourself from it. The Jewish sage of the Middle Ages, Moses Maimonides, wrote that, "He who destroys himself, destroys the world." Centuries later the German Enlightenment philosopher Immanuel Kant wrote, similarly, that suicide is wrong

6.   Ludwig Wittgenstein, *Notebooks* (Chicago: University of Chicago Press, 1984), p. 91.

because to destroy oneself destroys a portion of human morality, as we are each a representative of morality in this otherwise unfair world. Schopenhauer had a nuanced position that can be understood as such: suicide is wrong because it fails – what we want to do is to destroy who we were, or destroy the whole world, and suicide does neither of these. Also, wrote Schopenhauer, the true "will" cannot destroy itself. Camus wrote that suicide is surrender to death, when what we should really be doing is rejecting death, even up to our final breath.

The reason we think that secularism should defend the right to suicide is largely because of a reaction against the religious prohibition. Before the Middle Ages, religion was relatively neutral on suicide – some, like Samson, were celebrated for it; while secularists tended to argue against it. Like Socrates, one of the other most famous suicides, Seneca, also was compelled to do it (by Emperor Nero), but wrote in his lifetime that it was wrong. He writes of having experienced a time of misery in which he was tempted to end his life, but consideration of the feelings of his aged father kept him from doing so. "I saw not my own courage in dying, but his courage broken by the loss of me. So I said to myself, 'You must live.' Sometimes even to live is an act of courage."[7]

For a while suicide was associated with religion, from the protest suicides of the Jews at Masada, to the suicide of Jesus and the martyrdom of so many of his followers. Martyrdom was at first a defense of the Jesus sect, illegal in the Roman world. Once Constantine made Christianity legal in 313, the martyrdom might have stopped, but it did not. The rage for martyrdom continued for centuries. As Christianity became more established martyrdom stopped seeming like a valiant defense of the religion and started to seem like an unnecessary tragedy. Losing its members this way no longer made sense for the Church. Efforts to quell the popularity of martyrdom resulted in the first general bans on suicide. In 305, the Council of Guadix actually amended its list of martyrs by deleting the names of all those who had died by their own hand. The 348 Council of Carthage went further than the Church had before, actively condemning all those who had chosen suicide under the pretext of piety, but had really done it for personal reasons.

Writing around 400, one of the great theologians of this early period of Christianity was Augustine of Hippo, North Africa, also known to us as Saint Augustine. Augustine made a point of asserting that Jesus' death was voluntary, writing, "His soul did not leave his body constrained, but because he would and where he would and how he would." Yet, he argued powerfully,

---

7.   Lucius Annaeus Seneca, *Letters to Lucilius*, trans. E. Phillips Barker (Oxford: Clarendon, 1932): II, 15.

that suicide was forbidden to all others. For the next thousand years the Church would continue to condemn suicide, escalating punishments from merely withholding a Christian burial, to actually torturing corpses, and denying families the right to inherit the suicide's estate. By the time of the European Enlightenment, secularists had long resented the Christian response to suicide. This was brought to its most famous expression in the work of philosophers David Hume and the Baron d'Holbach. Neither really considered the meaning of suicide for a person, his or her family, friends, and community. Instead, they joked and railed against the idea that a God had forbid it. Ever since these arguments it has seemed that secularism sided with the right to suicide.

The idea that secularists are in favor of the right to suicide is part of the culture of secularism and should be open to fresh consideration. Like religion, secular culture has beliefs that become calcified and ritualized. Even religions reconsider their beliefs and behaviors from time to time, but for secularists the willingness to do so is a central feature of our ideology.

Some of what inhibits us from re-examining our values is that secularism in the early twenty-first century is too narrowly associated with science. To be sure, there have been artists and writers who used their work to celebrate religion, but through history there have also been many who used art as a way to explore the human experience on its own terms. Sometimes they were explicit that they became artists because they did not believe in religion's world-fixing propositions and were therefore driven to come to terms with the world as it is.

One of the greatest poets in the English language, Percy Bysshe Shelley, was also one of the great atheists of his age. As a young man, Shelley was kicked out of Oxford University for having written and (anonymously) distributed a tract called, "The Necessity of Atheism," in which he asserted that atheism was the only reasonable position. His poetry was not generally about atheism, but rather about life. His sonnet "Ozymandias," for example, speaks of wandering in the desert and coming upon a colossal broken statue of a great ruler, in pieces and strewn about half-buried in the sand. On the pedestal these words appear: "My name is Ozymandias, king of kings, look on my works ye mighty and despair." Then Shelley tells us "nothing besides remains" all around "the lone and level sands stretch far away." The works mentioned on the pedestal – presumably an impressive civilization – have been eaten by time. The poem is about the immensity of time in comparison to the life span of human beings and their accomplishments, even when those accomplishments seem massive and lasting from our point of view.

Religious people can respond to that shocking reality by denying it – claiming for instance that the world is 6,000 years old – and/or by speaking of a God who essentially humanizes eternity. What Shelley does, instead, is to accept and marvel at the strange sense of disjuncture between the human experience of time and the time frames of the earth, the galaxy, and the universe. Crucially, it is not just what Shelley says, but the fact that he said it so beautifully. Even as he is despairing of human plans and projects, he creates a thing of beauty so well made that 200 years later (the poem was first published in 1818) we still cherish it. The culture reproduces it in a thousand places and I, for one, have known every word of it since I was a child. Despairing of human permanence, he yet participated in it. Aware of the meaning rupture between cosmic time and human time, he finds beauty in it.

Living well as a human being requires participation in culture. Even a person who chooses to live alone on a mountaintop, with no books or music, is aware of the cultural invention of this kind of solitude and meditation.

We cannot escape culture, nor fully avoid the meaning it offers, but that does not mean it all comes easy. Living in a sense of meaning requires some effort. The human experience includes sorrow, alienation, frustration, and disappointment. Secularists do not care for the word "faith" but it seems to me that we need to work on our faith in humanity and meaning in the same way that believers have to work on their faith in God. It is hard to have faith that human life is meaningful, that human beings are willing to help one another and are capable of doing so, but at least they exist.

It may seem odd to encourage belief in something, but consider the experience of love. All sorts of evidence show us that sustaining long-term relationships make us happy, and all sorts of evidence show us that this is not easy. We fall in romantic love without much effort and we are born with a capacity to love our family members, but sometimes we tire of these relationships and have to sustain them across periods of dissatisfaction. We work on our marriages. We work to maintain our friendships. We forgive our family members and swallow our anger over and over in order to have them in our lives, in one way or another. Love is not scientific, nor is it always evident, but we know it is real because we feel it and we know of it from the culture around us. So we work on it. The meaning of life is like this. We feel it sometimes. We also know it from other people, and from art. If we want to feel it more of the time, we have to work on it.

Speaking this way is so out of favor that I have given it a name, "Poetic Atheism," to make it easier to advocate for it. It has always been around. Indeed, many of the prominent atheists of our time have expressed ideas of poetic atheism at times. Carl Sagan famously explained that all of the materials in our bodies come from exploding stars and therefore "We're made of star-stuff." It is a beautifully poetic notion. I'm arguing that we need to think more about the poetics of human existence, and to thereby have a secularism that helps us to live. Not everyone will agree with my anti-suicide argument, but I hope we can agree that the conversation is worth having. Our morality is not settled, it is open for revision and improvement, and recognizing how we manage our absurd human experience is a necessary part of that.

When we get over our God hangover and start seeing the human heart and mind within the immense universe, with no hidden supernatural force to reconcile them, we can rise to the challenge of our innate sense of justice and our capacity for empathy.

We live in a harsh world that is also full of warmth and affection, passion and Eros, love and empathy, dedication and virtue. It is a caustic world, and rare is the latitude in which we need neither coat nor sunscreen, rare the community in which we get everything we feel we need. Yet everywhere we find some love and mutuality, beauty and joy. The meaning rupture never goes away entirely, but we can see our own complex selves reflected in its paradox and work to make the human world as rich and strange as we desire.

2 Humanism and the Conquest of Fear

Dale McGowan[*]

In the north of England, beneath the amber waters of the River Tees, lives a creature by the name of Peg Powler. Peg is a mermaid – not the perky little teenage redhead of the Disney film, with her clamshell bikini and lovestruck eyes, but a river hag, with green hair and skin and a row of jagged teeth flashing like knives. Unlike Ariel, Peg lives not to make children glad but to kill and eat them.

Peg Powler lives in the foamy yellow rapids of the river. "Wander too close to the river's edge," goes the mother's warning, "especially near that foam, and Peg will have you by the ankle. She'll yank you below the water and eat you up, flesh, bones, and all." To drive the point home, Peg is said to end the gruesome meal with a ghastly belch of yellow foam.

The Tees is no meandering stream. Dropping from its rugged source on Cross Fell at a rate 20 times faster than the Thames, it roars through narrow, rocky vales to produce coursing rapids and three of the most impressive waterfalls in Britain – Low Force, High Force, and Cauldron Snout. In addition to the fast current, the water is very, very cold. It's this feature that causes someone falling into the water to inhale in a sudden gasp upon contact, one of the most common causes of drowning. Add the fact that the Tees runs as much as 15 feet deep with intense undercurrents, and drownings are a logical but tragic drumbeat throughout the river's course and history.

So it comes as no surprise that the legend of Peg Powler was born on the banks of the Tees rather than the sluggish Thames. The creature was clearly

[*] Dale McGowan is editor and co-author of *Raising Freethinkers* (2009) and *Parenting Beyond Belief* (2007) and the anthology *Voices of Unbelief* (2011), and author of *Atheism for Dummies* (2013) and *In Faith and in Doubt* (2014). He currently serves as founding executive director of Foundation Beyond Belief, a non-profit organization focusing, encouraging, and demonstrating humanist generosity and volunteerism. Dale holds degrees in physical anthropology and music from UC Berkeley and the University of Minnesota. In 2008, he was named Harvard Humanist of the Year.

imagined into existence for one purpose only – to scare children safe. She is naturally said to live in the foam, which marks the most dangerously turbulent spots in the river. And the occasional drowning reinforces and perpetuates the legend. Peg will have her meal.

Wherever there are parents and water, such legends find fertile soil. Inuit Islanders in Alaska warn their children of Tizheruk, an enormous sea snake said to snatch children from shore with its tail. Serbs tell of Bukavac, a six-legged lake-dweller that jumps from the water to strangle passersby – and again, a culinary preference is expressed for the young. Even as water-starved a region as aboriginal Australia has a water-dwelling child-eater called the *muldjewangk* living in the Murray, one of the few major rivers on the continent.

There are childhood dangers other than water, of course. Slavic mothers have traditionally warned their little ones not to wander off in public places for fear of Baba Yaga, a witch who preys specifically on lost children. Dropping from the sky in a flying mortar and pestle, Baba sweeps the lost ones off their feet and takes them to her hut on chicken legs, which is surrounded by a fence built from the bones of her tiny victims. In Upper Egypt, parents warn of the monstrous *silowa*, which is said to pass through villages from its home in the hills at dusk to get a drink at the Nile, dining on children along the way. This by itself would be no more extreme than any of the monsters invoked above, but the landscape of fear for rural Egyptian children extends far beyond specific physical protections into a network of superstitious horrors. Children are warned not to look at their own shadows lest they go insane and are instructed to chant passages from the Qur'an whenever passing "haunted places" – which according to some observers seem to occur every ten steps in most villages. Kenyan toddlers who will not nurse are set outside in the dark while the mother calls loudly from the hut for the *manani* (wild beasts) to come and eat the child.

Eucalyptus trees in Australia – called "widow-makers" for their tendency to suddenly lose enormous branches – are said to shelter vicious man-eating koalas called "drop bears" for their practice of dropping and dining on those who camp beneath the tree. The child-munching *hiisi* of Finland live in and around crevasses, large boulders, and the edges of cliffs; and the Polish ghoul *Południca* causes children trespassing in cornfields to become forever lost among the stalks.

And so it goes on, in every culture and every time. We populate an already frightening world with useful monsters, hoping to bring ill-defined risks into focus, keeping the most vulnerable among us safe – terrified, perhaps, but alive.

Warning legends such as these tend to involve a kind of cost-benefit analysis: The cost to the child in fear and mental anguish is weighed against the potential for harm, and the benefit of protection – from dangers real or parentally imagined – almost always wins. This is not a conscious process, but a subconscious cultural calculus by which a monster's terrors are equated to a danger in the parents' eyes.

But protective monsters have one very serious failing: they are often specific, while the danger they represent is general. A child who learns to fear Peg Powler will not necessarily generalize the danger to other rivers, much less to other risks. On a visit to the River Spey in Scotland – no less dangerous but free of the peat-stained yellow foam – a child raised to watch for Peg might happily tempt the waters, since the fearful hag is so very far away. By misrepresenting the danger, it could be argued that specific supernatural protection myths make children *less* safe than a reasoned description of real dangers. And recent advances in neurology, psychology, and social sciences suggest with ever-greater clarity that a fear-based approach to parenting or education is among the least effective options at our disposal. It works in limited, short-term ways and fails as a solution to the more general long-term problems for which parents must prepare their children. But again and again, generation after generation, the easy fix of fear is the very first option we consider, the very first tool we reach for. The result is a sobering paradox: continuous anxiety, and the naming or personification of evil, makes us feel vigilant and therefore safe, while in fact distracting us and making us less safe.

All of the useful monsters above serve the admirable purpose of protecting children from potentially lethal harm. While an argument can be made for allowing kids to make mistakes and learn from them, there's little point in advocating the occasional slip into a fast-moving river as a lesson in avoiding danger. There's a very real chance that no further opportunities to use that wisdom will present themselves.

The problem is in the next step. Having found fear a useful tool for protecting children from harm, adults have then found it difficult to resist using fear as a tool of control—not only for children, but for each other.

Why We Fear

> The brain is an inelegant and inefficient agglomeration of stuff… Evolution is a tinkerer, not an engineer… The brain is built like an ice cream cone (and you are the top scoop): Through evolutionary time, as higher functions were added, a new scoop was placed on top, but the lower scoops were left largely unchanged. David Linden, *The Accidental Mind.*

To understand why fear plays such a major role in human life, there's no better place to look than the Paleolithic Era (2.4 million years ago – 11,000 years ago). Over 99.5 percent of the history of the genus *Homo* – 120,000 generations – took place during the Paleolithic. For the last 10,000 of those generations, we were anatomically modern. Same body, same brain. The brain you are carrying around in your head was evolved in response to conditions in that era, not this one. The mere 500 generations that have passed since the Paleolithic ended represent a virtual goose egg in evolutionary time.

To put it simply: we are born in the Stone Age. Childhood is a period during which we are brought – by parenting, experience, and education – into the modern world. Or not.

So if we were evolved for the Paleolithic, it seems worth asking: what was it like then? In short, it was miserable to be us.

In the Lower Paleolithic, starting around 2.4 million years ago, there were an estimated 26,000 hominids on Earth. The climate was affected by frequent glacial periods that would lock up global water, leading to severe arid conditions in the temperate zones and scarce plant and animal life, making food hard to come by.

The average hominid life span was about 22 years. We lived in small bands competing for negligible resources. For two million years, our genus balanced on the razor's edge of extinction.

Then it got worse. About 77,000 years ago, a supervolcano erupted in what is now Lake Toba in Indonesia. On the Volcanic Explosivity Index (which was apparently created by a seven-year-old boy), this eruption was a "mega-colossal" — the highest category. Earth was plunged into a volcanic winter lasting at least a decade. The human population dropped to an estimated 5,000 individuals, each living a terrifying, marginal existence.

This terrifying, marginal existence bequeathed some unfortunate human tendencies. Because food was desperately hard to come by, cooperation within a small group was advantageous, but cooperating with the group next door would have doubled the mouths to feed without moving the needle much on available food. Genetic tendencies toward in-group cooperation and out-group hostility would have provided a selective advantage, as would distrust of people who dressed, looked, or acted differently from you. The more different they were, the more likely their interests conflicted with yours.[1]

Aggressive nationalism, militarism, racism, and an exaggerated fear of immigrants and of all things foreign – these are modern expressions of what

1.   For a marvelous exploration of this idea, see ch. 6 of Richard Dawkins' *The Selfish Gene* (Oxford: Oxford University Press, 1989).

was once a sensible approach to staying alive. But in an interdependent world, these same characteristics can be harmful.

Our evolved tendency goes well beyond the fear of each other to the fear of pretty much everything. And this is indeed an evolved tendency, meaning it does – or at least *did* – confer a selective advantage.

It's easy to understand why. Imagine it's a sunny Wednesday afternoon a million years ago. Two *Homo erectus* are walking through the high grass on the African savannah. Suddenly there's movement off to the left. One of them assumes it's something fun and goes in for a hug. The other jumps straight up 15 feet and grabs a tree limb. Even if it's just a fluffy bunny nine times out of ten, which of these guys is more likely to pass on his genes to the next generation?

In a world bent on killing you, no characteristic would have been more useful for survival than perpetual, sweaty hyper-vigilance. We've inherited a strong tendency to assume that every shadow and sound is a threat, which in turn kept us alive and reproducing. By the time elevated blood pressure killed you off at 22, you'd already have several jittery, paranoid offspring pounding espressos and cradling stone shotguns all through the long, terrifying night.

Now remember that these humans had the same thirsty and capable brain you and I enjoy, but few reliable methods for filling it up. The most common cause of death was infectious disease. If someone is gored by a mammoth, you can figure out how to avoid that in the future. But most people died for no apparent reason. They just broke out in bloody boils, then keeled over dead.

Imagine how terrifying such a world would be to a mind fully *capable* of comprehending the situation but utterly lacking in answers, and worse yet, lacking the ability to control it. It's not hard to picture the human mind simply rebelling against that reality, declaring it unacceptable, and creating an alternate reality in its place, neatly packaged for the grateful relief of subsequent generations. Evil can't be banished, so instead it was named and personified. Baba Yaga. Peg Powler. Satan.

Surely it's no coincidence that the first evidence of supernatural religion, the packaging of an alternate reality more bearable than the real thing, appears 130,000 years ago, right in the Paleolithic midst.

Religion solves our central problem: that we are human (to quote Jennifer Hecht), and the universe is not. It's not really about explanation or even comfort, not exactly. It's about seizing control, or at least imagining we have. To be fully conscious of our frailty and mortality in a hostile and indifferent universe and powerless to do anything about it would have been simply unacceptable to the human mind. So we created powerful beings that we could ultimately control — through prayer, sacrifice, behavior changes, ritual, spinning around three times, what have you.

Conservative, traditional religion is a natural response to being human in the Paleolithic. Whether it's a good response or not is beside the point — it was the only one we had.

"But we're not in the Paleolithic anymore," you say. You certainly have the calendar on your side. We began to climb out of our situation about 500 generations ago when agriculture made it possible to stand still and live a little longer. Eventually we had the time and security to develop better responses to the problem, better ways of interrogating and controlling the world around us. But the Scientific Revolution, our biggest step forward in that journey, was just 20 generations ago. Think of that. It *just* happened. Our species is still suffering from the post-traumatic stress of 120,000 generations in hell. And like the battle veteran who hits the dirt when he hears a backfiring car, it takes very little to push the Paleolithic button in our heads.

Parenting Away the Paleolithic

Yes, our kids are born without religious belief. But they are also born with the problem of being human, which includes a strong tendency to hit the dirt when the universe backfires. In a world of seven billion people in close quarters, it's no longer quite so adaptive to have everybody all edgy and shooty all the time. But our brains don't know that. One of the resulting paradoxes is that fear often increases as actual danger diminishes. If you can't see and name it, we figure it must be hiding, which is ever so much worse. Violent crime in the United States recently hit the lowest level[2] since records have been kept – in *every* category – but who'd ever know? Instead, we take every violent news story as proof of the opposite. We insist things are worse than ever in "this day and age," keep cradling those shotguns… and keep forwarding those urban legends.

When you get an email warning that rapists are using $5 bills or recordings of crying babies or ether disguised as perfume to lure and capture their victims, or that child abduction rates have risen 444 percent since 1982 – all untrue – you've just received an email from the Paleolithic. But by constantly naming dangers and sounding the alarm, we feel safer.

Think for a minute about how the attacks of September 11, 2001 – a death-dealing sneak attack by the "Other" – pushed our collective Paleolithic button. It was a massive confirmation of our oldest unarticulated fears, and we dropped to our collective knees.

2.   US Bureau of Justice Statistics, http://www.bjs.gov/content/glance/viort.cfm.

In addition to magical thinking, fear of difference, and hyper-vigilance, we can add categorical thinking, enforced gender divisions, the love of weapons and authority, and much more, all of which had clear adaptive advantages during the long, dark night of our species. These things are, in a word, natural.

Which is not to say good. Rape is also natural. "From an evolutionary perspective," says biologist/philosopher David Lahti, "considering other social species on this earth, it is remarkable that a bunch of unrelated adult males can sit on a plane together for seven hours in the presence of fertile females, with everyone arriving alive and unharmed at the end of it."[3] Yet it happens, ten thousand times a day, because we've developed a frankly unnatural social morality that trumps the natural a gratifyingly high percentage of the time.

Secularism, comfort with difference, a reasonable relaxation of vigilance, the blurring of categories (sex, gender, race), the willingness to disarm ourselves and to challenge authority – these are all unnatural, recent developments, born in fits and starts out of the relative luxury of a post-Paleolithic world. I'm sure you'll agree that they are also *better* responses to the world we live in now – at least those of us privileged to live in non-Paleolithic conditions.

Of course our limbic brain differs on that, but it would, wouldn't it?

Now – the astute reader may have noticed that the things that kept us alive a million years ago line up incredibly well with the nationalistic, anti-immigrant, pro-gun, pro-authority, pro-gender-role, anti-diversity talking points of social conservatives. But if you think my point is to belittle conservatives by calling them cavemen, not so. I think there's a lot to be gained by recognizing social conservatism, including religious conservatism, as the activation of ancient and natural fears, and to respond accordingly – and humanistically.

The fear of difference that fuels racism, xenophobia, and militarism is not just unnecessary now – in a world as interdependent as ours, it's actually maladaptive. But too little time has passed for our new situation to rewire the human brain.

Adding to the problem of fearing irrelevant things is our failure to fear relevant ones – to recognize *real* threats here in the twenty-first century. We feel sick with fear on the observation desk of a skyscraper, even if a high rail holds us back, because our brains are still very much in the treetops. That healthy fear of high places kept our ancestors alive long enough to become our ancestors and pass the fear to us.

3.   Lahti, David. "Why Does Religion Keep Telling Us We're Bad?" *The Guardian* (UK), Nov 22, 2011.

We still jump when we see a snake two feet away, even if it's behind glass at the zoo. But on the way home from the zoo, we'll hurtle along at 70 miles an hour in a tin box without a seatbelt while texting and feel no fear. Natural selection hasn't had time to vote on texting behind the wheel yet.

Give it time.

We're not working too hard to abandon those ancient fears because there is that paradoxical way in which being afraid makes us feel safer.

Picture a tense movie in which the hero, gun at the ready, his face tense, works his way slowly through the abandoned warehouse, backing around stacks of boxes. He swings around the final corner and sweeps the area with his gun extended. All is clear. He breathes a sigh of relief and holsters his gun. His face falls into casual relaxation.

And you *know* what's coming next. As long as he was intense, focused, vigilant, afraid, he was safe. The moment he lets down his guard, that's when the evil will strike.

Film-makers know that this narrative is woven into us. Our savannah-dwelling selves see danger lurking in every shadow. If we are afraid, if we are ever vigilant, we are safe. If we relax, we die. So a constant state of fear is our natural condition. We cling to it. We seek out new ways to be afraid. It makes us feel that we have named the evil in the world and we are therefore in control of it.

The irony here is that most Americans live in a bubble of physical safety unprecedented in human history. Average life expectancy in developed countries has doubled in 100 years. And despite the constant claim that violent crime has never been worse, the constant warning that you can't be too careful in "this day and age," those bottoming rates of violent crime show that we have literally never been safer from each other.

It's not just a matter of "Who would ever know?" but "Who *wants* to know?" There is a very real way in which our vigilance requires us to be under assault. So we live our lives in a state of orange alert and encourage our kids to do the same. My friends and loved ones receive a frantic email warning of pedophiles on Facebook, or terrorists on the PTA, and they believe it, and they forward it to everyone they know, and having named the evil, they feel safer. This is the small scale, of course. The same desire to identify a boogeyman that is responsible for all of our troubles has led historically to racial hatred, warfare, and genocide.

If a state of constant fear added to the quality of our lives, if it made this world a better place, I'd say why not. Let's be afraid, all the time. But a growing body of research shows just why we need to start seeing our addiction to fear as a problem.

It turns out that when we are afraid, we are more selfish, less generous. We are less empathetic. We are more likely to respond aggressively and to assume the worst in ambiguous situations. We are less tolerant of difference and less patient. We are more likely to behave both unreasonably and unethically.

To turn these tendencies around, reduce fear.

My Lucky Virtue

By all accounts I'm a tolerant, ethical, non-aggressive person. I'd take a bow, but I don't think I deserve too much credit for those things, and my deflection has nothing to do with false modesty. Most of the credit goes to the fact that I've experienced much less fear and insecurity in my life than most people on Earth, especially when I was young. My circumstances allowed my Paleolithic buttons to remain unpushed. That's why I'm not a social conservative. That's why valuing and accepting diversity are no-brainers for me. Growing up, I was made to feel safe. I was not frightened with Satan or hell or made to question my own worth or worthiness. I was given an education, allowed to think freely, encouraged to explore the world around me and to find it wonderful. Unlike the vast majority of the friends I have who are religious conservatives, I never passed through a disempowering life crisis – a hellish divorce, a drug or alcohol spiral, the loss of a child – that may have triggered that feeling of abject helplessness before I had developed my own personal resources to deal with such calamities. So I never had to retreat into the cave of my innate fears.

In short, I've been damn lucky.

That luck doesn't always lead to secular humanism. A lot of people with the same luck are religious. But in my experience, those strongly tend toward what social commentator Bruce Bawer has called the "church of love" – the tolerant, diverse, justice-oriented side of the religious spectrum, grounded in a more modern perspective but still responding to the human problem that science, admittedly, has only partly solved.

It's rare for a person with all of the advantages listed above to freely choose the "church of law" – the narrow, hateful, Paleolithic end we rightly oppose. Those folks, one way or another, are generally thrown there. Sometimes they find their way out, but their road is tougher than mine was.

Seeing things this way has made me more empathetic to conservative religious believers, even as I oppose the malign consequences of their beliefs. Understanding our natural inheritance also makes me frankly amazed that we ever do *anything* right. Given the profound mismatch between what we are and what the world is, we should all have vanished in a smoking heap by now. Instead, we create art and cure disease and write symphonies and figure out the age of the universe and somehow, despite ourselves, hang on to an essentially secular government in a predominantly religious country.

Religious and social conservatism are symptoms of our ancient fears, reactions to the problem of being a Stone Age human. For the half of the planet still living in marginal conditions, that problem is mostly unsolved. For the rest of us – thanks to agriculture, germ theory, separating our drinking water from our poop, the scientific method, and a thousand other advances, we've made some serious progress. And that partial solution has made all the difference, freeing us up to live better lives than we once did.

As a humanist parent, one of the best things I can do for the world at large is to teach my kids that the Paleolithic is over.

Education, experience, and parenting take a child from Stone Age newborn to modern adult in about 6,000 days. Or so we hope. In addition to shoe tying, the five-paragraph essay, algebra, good oral hygiene, the age of the universe, the French Revolution, and how to boil an egg, there's something else we need to help them learn, or better yet, *feel* – that life is better and you have more control than your factory settings would have you believe.

At a freethought convention several years ago, author/film-maker (and Darwin great-great-grandson) Matthew Chapman was asked why Europe rapidly secularized after the Second World War while the United States remained devout. He paused for a moment. "Honestly," he said, "I think socialized medicine had a lot to do with it."

Not the answer we were expecting.

For most of the history of our species, he said, we've been haunted by an enormous sense of personal insecurity, and for good reason. The threat of death or incapacity was always hanging over us. Religion offered a sense of security, the illusion of control. Once the states of Europe began to relieve some of those basic fears, people began to feel a greater sense of control and security, and the need for traditional religion began to wane.

Whether that's the whole answer or not, I think he's on to something here. Traditional religion is driven by human insecurity. I have a good number of friends and relations in the deep and toxic end of the religious pool, and I can't think of one who truly jumped in unpushed. Some were born into it and raised to believe they couldn't live without it. Other experienced some kind of life crisis resulting in a terrifying loss of control that pushed those ancient buttons – and they jumped in with both feet.

I feel immense empathy for these people – even when their beliefs make me nauseous.

I also have many friends who genuinely chose religion instead of needing it. And lo and behold, these folks tend to end up in more liberal expressions, doing little harm and a lot of good. They aren't hostages to their innate fears. In fact, they have a lot more in common with me than with the people hyperventilating and clinging to Jesus in the deep end.

I really don't care if my kids end up identifying with religion so long as it's a *choice*, not a *need*. And the best way I can ensure that is by using these 6,000 days to give them not just knowledge but also *confidence and security.*

Turns out we know how to do this. You start with a sensitive, responsive, and consistent home life. Build a strong attachment with parents and other significant adults. Don't hit or humiliate them or let others do so. Encourage them to challenge authority, including your own. Make them comfortable with difference. Use knowledge to drive out fear. Build a sense of curiosity and wonder that will keep them self-educating for life. Let them know that your love and support are unconditional. Teach and expect responsibility and maturity. Encourage self-reliance. Help them find and develop "flow" activities and lose themselves in them.

These aren't off the top of my head, you know – they're straight out of the best child development research, which strongly supports attachment theory and authoritative parenting. Bottom line is, the best practices for humanist parenting are in sync with the best practices for...parenting. Just like the best practices for being a humanist are in sync with the best practices for being a human.

Conservative religious parents have to close their eyes and swim hard upstream against this research consensus, following James Dobson *et al.* back to the Paleolithic. But liberal religious parents, who share most of my parenting goals, have the same advantage I do. They can even claim one of the foremost advocates of attachment theory as their own – William Sears, a sane and sensible Christian parenting author who opposes almost every major parenting position of James Dobson.

The Central Task of Humanism

So much of the poison we inflict on each other is rooted in fear. Humanism at its best is about helping ourselves and others transcend the paralyzing fears we have inherited. That's why my daily practice as a humanist rarely involves shouting, arguing, or assailing the less humane ideas of others. It's not because I think those ideas merit my respect. It's because it is so rarely effective. I know those ideas are rooted in fear, and that the attack more often than not is counterproductive, driving people ever deeper into their fearful shells. Instead, the primary task of the humanist should be lifting people up, encouraging them, strengthening them, relaxing their ancient vigilance so they can set aside those unworthy ideas and find their own way forward – not because it's "nice," but because it has a much better chance of changing the world.

When atheists and humanists recognize that our naturalistic worldview has less to do with our intelligence than with the lucky circumstances that have lifted us out of the terrors we inherited, our next step becomes clear – turn around, in empathy and compassion, and offer a hand to those who are still immersed in those terrors, still mesmerized and controlled by them. If you want to fight ignorance, division, violence, and every form of inhumanity, don't use a sledgehammer on the symptoms. Go to the root causes that push those ancient buttons and make us feel our vulnerability so intensely. Fight poverty. Work for universal health care. Insist on basic human rights. When we move beyond the intellectual to make these things an essential part of the daily practice of humanism, we'll find the toxic residue of our abused past falling away faster than argumentation ever could achieve.

3   The Humanist Case for Cooperation

Chris Stedman*

Cooperating in Moorhead, Minnesota

In my first ever piece for *The Huffington Post Religion*, published in 2010, I wrote about Moorhead, Minnesota-based Concordia College's refusal to recognize "Secular Students of Concordia," an organization for nontheist students.[1] In that piece I argued that, in order to be truly inclusive, interfaith efforts must also include – and stand up for – those without faith, who are often marginalized and discriminated against in the United States and around the world.[2]

The debate about giving Concordia's nonreligious population official recognition and a voice on campus first began in November 2009, when a group of students applied to form Secular Students of Concordia. The group's stated goal was to be "a secular alternative to the religious and faith

*   Chris Stedman is Coordinator of Humanist Life at Yale University and former Assistant Humanist Chaplain at Harvard University. He received his Master's in Religion (Pastoral Care and Counseling) from Meadville Lombard Theological School. Additionally, he received a Bachelor of Arts in Religion from Augsburg College in Minnesota. Stedman is the Emeritus Managing Director of State of Formation at the Journal of Inter-Religious Dialogue, a website for emerging religious and ethical thinkers. He writes for *Huffington Post Gay Voices*, *Huffington Post Religion*, *The Washington Post On Faith*, *Religion Dispatches*, *Relevant*, and other publications on issues relating to atheism and interfaith dialogue. Most recently, he wrote a book on his experiences as an atheist and interfaith activist called *Faitheist: How an Atheist Found Common Ground with the Religious* (2012).

1.   Some portions of this essay previously appeared online or are adapted from Chris Stedman, *Faitheist: How an Atheist Found Common Ground with the Religious* (Boston: Beacon Press, 2012) and are reprinted by permission of Beacon Press. Thanks to Andreas Rekdal, Chelsea Link, Stephen Goeman, Vlad Chituc, and others for insights and feedback.
2.   Robert Evans, "U.N. Told Atheists Face Discrimination around Globe," *Reuters*, February 25, 2013, http://www.reuters.com.

based clubs at Concordia."[3] Their application was rejected by the school on the grounds that "the organization [was] not in compliance with ELCA [the Evangelical Lutheran Church of America] and the College Standards."

Looking at the organization's constitution, a few aspects appeared problematic with regard to the college's non-discrimination policies and religious affiliation. For example: by approving the Secular Students of Concordia, the college itself could have potentially placed itself in a position of being forced to make a donation to the self-described "aggressive, in-your-face"[4] American Atheists, a national organization widely known for its confrontational tactics and anti-religious activism – a perhaps less-than-tempting prospect for a college that finds itself at the crossroads of its increasingly religiously diverse student body and its explicitly Christian heritage. In January 2011 the group's founder Bjørn Kvernstuen appealed against the college's decision and reapplied for recognition with a redrafted constitution that removed many of the problematic elements, but the college rejected this application as well.

Ironically, the resistance met by the Secular Students of Concordia coincided with a campus-wide push for interfaith dialogue and cooperation. A group of students began forming a "Better Together" interfaith campaign affiliated with the national interfaith movement-building organization Interfaith Youth Core (IFYC), and the college was in the process of creating a campus office concerned with matters of interfaith cooperation and community service. Moreover, the following academic year kicked off with an appeal for interfaith dialogue in a September 2012 campus-wide lecture by IFYC founder Eboo Patel.

Interpreting the choice of Patel as the convocation speaker as an invitation for religious minorities to become part of the larger discussion on interfaith, another group of students submitted an intent form for an organization they called the "Secular Student Community" in October 2012. This organization was meant to be a place of belonging for Concordia's many nonreligious students, centered around constructive dialogue about humanist morality. Furthermore, the group wished to spark a campus-wide conversation about inclusivity – to raise awareness about the college's nontheist students, and to advocate on their behalf.

3.   This information, and much of the following information about this incident, is courtesy of Andreas Rekdal and Kristi Del Vecchio, graduates of Concordia College who were involved in the efforts to establish a secular student group on campus as students.
4.   American Atheists, Inc, Facebook.com, March 9, 2012, http://www.facebook.com/AmericanAtheists/posts/10150643252207418.

Six months later – to the surprise of many – the group gained official recognition from the college. What had changed from 2010 to 2013 that allowed for this?

Significantly, nonreligious students had become interfaith leaders. In fact, atheists, agnostics and humanists were significantly represented in Concordia's interfaith group, which was led by the school's most outspoken atheist, Kristi Del Vecchio. These students saw the value of interfaith dialogue for all people – atheists included – and decided to become active proponents of interfaith dialogue on campus. Likewise, religious students involved in interfaith efforts at Concordia stepped out and used their voices to be vital allies for the nonreligious.

Recognizing nonreligious students' desire to build relationships and be part of the discussion about religion at Concordia, and that they had the support of many of their religious peers, administrators and faculty began to reach out. The chairperson of Concordia's Religion department called administrators to ask why the Secular Student Community's application process was taking so long. Concordia's Campus Ministries invited Del Vecchio to speak during interfaith chapel week. Using the opportunity to clear the air about stereotypes surrounding atheism and emphasizing the common ground she sees between herself and her religious peers, Kristi helped spark a renewed discussion around the role of the nonreligious within the institution.

Shortly after I visited Concordia to talk about Humanism and interfaith work, meet with students, and speak with administrators about the need to support all students, the Secular Student Community – an organization similar in name and still centered around nontheistic identity and humanistic values like the group that preceded it, but with a different vision – was approved. This affirmation of secular students' place within an otherwise predominantly religious institution owes largely to precisely the kind of interfaith dialogue and collaboration I called for in my 2010 piece about the initial group's rejection – the kind of approach that encourages mutual respect and solidarity between atheists and the religious, rather than scorn or derision.

With this decision, Concordia's students, faculty, and administration demonstrated that, in a world fixated on culture wars and disagreements, there is another way forward for atheists and the religious – one defined by mutual respect and support, rather than condescension or dismissal – that can lead us to a religiously pluralistic society.

What is Religious Pluralism? Is it a Humanist Value?

Religious pluralism is neither coexistence nor consensus. IFYC's Eboo Patel and Cassie Meyer write: "Drawing from Harvard scholar Diana Eck, IFYC articulates religious pluralism as the active engagement of religious diversity to a constructive end. Diversity is a mere descriptive fact; 'pluralism is an achievement' (Eck). We break this definition further into three essential components: respect for individual religious or non-religious identity, mutually inspiring relationships, and common action for the common good."[5]

Interfaith dialogue strives to usher in religious pluralism, and it is realized primarily through the personal stories of its practitioners. Storytelling aids dialogue because it is non-threatening, prompts a mutual exchange of stories that help people bond, and allows people to talk about their identities in a way that feels safe. By grounding dialogue in individual experience, the listener is less likely to be offended by what might be alien to her or his own experience. Instead of provoking a negative response, IFYC suggests that this exchange can result in mutually inspiring relationships and common action:

> While [a participant] may not have lived the same experience as the storyteller, it is unlikely that they will challenge the veracity of his or her own story. Instead, the storyteller is inviting the listeners to share in a piece of his or her own experience, even if it is grounded in different beliefs or values. The dialogue is therefore inclusive rather than exclusive and allows for a mutually appreciative encounter.[6]

Before one can become an active agent of engaging religious diversity, an individual must be grounded in her or his own particular story and identity. This of course presents two intriguing questions: How might humanists participate in a movement encouraging engaged religious pluralism that is rooted in particular religious identity? And why should we?

I. Five Reasons Humanists Should Engage

There are five primary reasons that engaging in interfaith work will benefit humanists, which I will expand on below: we're outnumbered; we want to end religious extremism and other forms of oppression and suffering; we have a lot to learn; we have a bad reputation and are discriminated against; and it is consistent with our humanist values.

---

5.   Eboo Patel and Cassie Meyer, "Defining Religious Pluralism: A Response to Robert McKim," *Journal of College and Character* 11.2 (2010), http://journals.naspa.org.

6.   IFYC, *The Interfaith Leader's Toolkit* (Chicago: IFYC, 2009), p. 16.

1. Nontheists are outnumbered, aka the pragmatic argument

Whether we wish to or not, atheists are forced by proximity to engage with the religious. We're outnumbered. Though the number of Americans who do not identify with any religion is growing, atheism and Humanism remain minority perspectives. More interestingly, American religious communities are undergoing some radical shifts that make it impossible for us to approach them as a monolithic and inert community that is strictly problematic.

While the percentage of Americans with no religious preference, often referred to as the "nones," has grown nearly five percentage points in the last five years, there are many possible reasons people might disaffiliate from religion. Some do not believe in religious claims – sure enough, 12 percent of the "nones" identify as atheist and 17 percent identify as agnostic. But for many, their lack of religious affiliation may have more to do with identity politics than belief. In fact, the majority of the religiously unaffiliated seem to carry some beliefs associated with traditionally religious thinking. Some 68 percent of nonreligious Americans claim to believe in a god or universal spirit (strangely, this includes 38 percent of atheists and agnostics), and 40 percent pray at least once a month. And though about 70 percent of them think religious organizations are too involved with money and politics, about 80 percent think that religious organizations help bring people together, build communities, and play an important role in helping the poor and those in need. To quote from Pew's report: "a majority of the religiously unaffiliated clearly think that religion can be a force for good in society."[7]

Additionally, while religious communities are becoming demonstratively more liberal, Pew's findings point to the fact that in many ways "Millennials remain fairly traditional in their religious beliefs and practices." Pew surveys have found that "young adults' beliefs about life after death and the existence of heaven, hell and miracles closely resemble the beliefs of older people today." Additionally, while Millennials pray less often than older generations today do, the number of Millennials who say they pray every day is on par with the number of young people who claimed to do so in previous generations; likewise, the number of Millennials who claim to believe in God with absolute certainty are consistent with the percentage among members of Generation X a decade ago.[8]

So while religion today looks very different than it has in the past, it isn't about to vanish from the face of the earth. And since religious believers

7.   "Religion among the Millennials," *Pew Research Religion and Public Life Project*, February 17, 2010, http://www.pewforum.org.
8.   "Religion among the Millennials."

are our neighbors, we ought to know them and their motivations. In giving them an opportunity to get to know us and the stories of our experiences as nonreligious persons – and, perhaps more importantly, not forgetting to get to know them – we will begin to erode some of the divisions between the secular and the religious. By doing so we are likely, as IFYC suggests, to identify some shared values upon which we can act in interfaith solidarity. The interfaith coalition that led the American civil rights movement recognized that success would require respecting the many different reasons people come to the table to support a common cause. Unless we strive to understand people's religious beliefs and practices, efforts that hinge on solidarity will fail. Without knowing and understanding the spectrum of moral and religious beliefs that compel people to act, we will remain divided.

You don't even need to think that religion can be a positive force in the world to see the value in interfaith cooperation that includes the nonreligious. As citizens of a religiously diverse world, interfaith cooperation is a necessity in order to accomplish things that require a coalition larger than the community to which you belong – whether you wish to see religion come to an end or not.

2. We want to end religious extremism and other forms of oppression and suffering, aka the shared-values argument

One such common goal shared by the interfaith cooperation movement and the atheist movement is a proactive aim to end religious extremism. The interfaith movement is inherently rooted in an anti-fundamentalism framework. In *Acts of Faith*, Eboo Patel writes that,

> the twenty-first century will be shaped by the question of the faith line. On one side of the faith line are the religious totalitarians. Their conviction is that only one interpretation of one religion is a legitimate way of being, believing, and belonging on earth. Everyone else needs to be cowed, or converted, or condemned, or killed. On the other side of the faith line are the religious pluralists, who hold that people believing in different creeds and belonging to different communities need to learn to live together.[9]

Humanists ought to see ourselves as having a lot in common with religious pluralists; likewise, religious pluralists are likely to see themselves as having more in common with us than with the extremists who also claim

9.   Eboo Patel, *Acts of Faith: The Story of an American Muslim, the Struggle for the Soul of a Generation* (Boston: Beacon, 2007), p. xv.

their tradition. In allying our efforts to combat religious extremism with like-minded campaigns occurring within religious communities, our efforts will be more effective. A Muslim speaking out against religious extremism will probably be better received by Muslim communities than would be a humanist.

In *Ethnic Conflict and Civic Life: Hindus and Muslims in India*, political scientist Ashutosh Varshney noted that the likelihood that inciting events will lead to widespread or long-term violence is significantly less in communities where civic ties across lines of identity differentiation were present.[10] In populations where such ties were non-existent, inciting incidents provoked extensive inter-identity violence. Thus, as interfaith cooperation asserts, invested relationships across lines of identity difference are essential for avoiding conflict.

One of the top priorities of humanist communities is criticizing and combating religiously based oppression, and pluralistic religious communities can be among our strongest allies in this work. However, if we adopt a broadly negative approach to religion and religious communities, we may burn these bridges and lose the opportunity to count these communities as allies.

3. We have a lot to learn, aka the educational argument

These mutual interests can never be identified if we fail to recognize that religious communities have a lot to teach us. In "E Pluribus Unum: Diversity and Community in the 21st Century,"[11] Robert Putnam wrote that diversity is important to building strong and sustainable communities. But, at least at first, people tend to "hunker down" with those very similar to themselves and gaze upon newcomers with suspicion. For diversity to flower, individuals must meet and learn from one another. As Carl Sagan once wrote: "Every one of us is, in the cosmic perspective, precious. If a human disagrees with you, let him live. In a hundred billion galaxies, you will not find another."[12]

While I agree with that sentiment, I'd like to go a step further. I don't want to just let those who disagree with me live – I want to go out of my way to try to befriend and understand them. Sure enough, some of my greatest insights have grown out of such relationships.

10.   Ashutosh Varshney, *Ethnic Conflict and Civic Life: Hindus and Muslims in India* (New Haven: Yale University Press, 2003).

11.   Robert D. Putnam, "E Pluribus Unum: Diversity and Community in the Twenty-First Century," The 2006 Johan Skytte Prize Lecture, *Scandinavian Political Studies*, Vol. 30, Issue 2 (June 15, 2007). Available at: http://onlinelibrary.wiley.com/doi/10.1111/j.1467-9477.2007.00176.x/full.

12.   Carl Sagan, *Cosmos* (New York: Random House, 1980), p. 339.

We can also learn from and adapt the best that religious communities have to offer, as Alain de Botton argued in *Religion for Atheists: A Non-Believer's Guide to the Uses of Religion*.[13] Furthermore, religious communities have often nurtured activists and anti-oppression movements. Many of history's greatest advocates for the disenfranchised – Reverend Dr Martin Luther King Jr, Mahatma Gandhi, Thich Nhat Hanh, Rabbi Abraham Joshua Heschel, Monseigneur Oscar Romero, and many others – cited their religious convictions as the primary impetus for their social justice work and launched their efforts in interfaith coalitions. And though some nontheists cast religion as an inherently bad thing, it is not difficult to make a case that aspects of religion have been and continue to be a force for good in the world. There is a storied history of religious social justice, and we would do well to learn from it; religiously based social justice continues in great force today, and we would do well to join with it. This will require a willingness to learn from people, even if we think some of their beliefs are incorrect.

It is also important to remember that religious criticism is not the exclusive domain of the nonreligious, and acting like it is by adopting a "religious people versus atheists" mentality while painting all religious believers with a broad brush alienates allies in the important fight against dogmatism and totalitarianism. Criticism of religious beliefs isn't a new thing; its legacy is as long as the existence of religion itself, and it rests on the backs of outspoken religious leaders like Martin Luther, Mahatma Gandhi, Martin Luther King Jr, and even the biblical Jesus Christ. But they – like many religious critics today who work within their own communities – were reformers, not abolitionists.

Regardless of whether you find anything in religion admirable, it seems that, for now anyway, religion is unlikely to become irrelevant. And in a world where religious conflict is in the headlines on a daily basis and religious illiteracy is widespread, it actually feels increasingly relevant. The dangers of acting like it isn't are clear: when fraught issues related to religion arise, being unable to contextualize them or understand their implications makes it difficult to know how to respond. Cultivating positive relationships between people of diverse religious and nonreligious identities not only helps prevent conflict by creating invested relationships – it also combats ignorance by giving people the opportunity to educate one another about their beliefs and backgrounds.

---

13.   Alain De Botton, *Religion for Atheists: A Non-believer's Guide to the Uses of Religion* (New York: Vintage, 2013).

4. We have a bad reputation and are discriminated against, aka the necessity argument

Because we represent such a small sliver of the American population – and because we are often seen in a negative light – it is imperative that atheists make themselves known. A 2010 Gallup poll demonstrated something the LGBTQ community has recognized for some time: people are significantly more inclined to oppose gay marriage if they do not know anyone who is gay.[14] Relationships can be transformative. The Pew Research Center found that among the 14 percent of Americans who changed their mind from opposing same-sex marriage to supporting it in the last decade, the top reason given was having "friends, family, acquaintances who are gay/ lesbian." Only two percent said that they changed their mind because they came to believe that gay and lesbian people are "born that way."[15] So while education is important, knowing someone of a different identity seems to be the key to change.

Similarly, a *Time* magazine cover story that same year featured revealing numbers that speak volumes about the correlation between positive relationships and civic support; per their survey, 46 percent of Americans think Islam is more violent than other faiths, and 61 percent oppose Park51 (or the so-called "Ground Zero Mosque"), but only 37 percent even know a Muslim American.[16] Another survey released around the same time, by Pew, reported that 55 percent of Americans know "not very much" or "nothing at all" about Islam. The disconnect is clear: when only 37 percent of Americans know a Muslim American, and 55 percent claim to know very little or nothing about Islam, the negative stereotypes about the Muslim community go unchallenged.[17]

The same logic can be extended to nontheists – the fewer relationships we have with people of faith, the worse our image will be. Based on my experiences as an atheist and an interfaith activist, I have confidence that building relationships of mutuality and respect will alter the negative public perceptions about atheists. As Abraham Lincoln once said:

14.   Lymari Morales, "Knowing Someone Gay/Lesbian Affects Views of Gay Issues," Gallup, May 29, 2009, http://www.gallup.com.

15.   "Changing Minds: Behind the Rise in Support for Gay Marriage," Pew Research Center for the People and the Press, March 21, 2013, http://people-press.org.

16.   Bobby Ghosh, "Mosque Controversy: Does America Have a Muslim Problem?" *Time*, August 30, 2010, http://www.time.com.

17.   "Public Remains Conflicted over Islam," Pew Research Center for the People and the Press, August 24, 2010, http://people-press.org.

If you would win a man to your cause, first convince him that you are his sincere friend. Therein is a drop of honey that catches his heart, which, say what he will, is the great high road to his reason, and which, when once gained, you will find but little trouble in convincing his judgment of the justice of your cause, if indeed that cause really be a just one. On the contrary, assume to dictate to his judgment, or to command his action, or to mark him as one to be shunned and despised, and he will retreat within himself, close all the avenues to his head and his heart; and tho' your cause be naked truth itself, transformed to the heaviest lance, harder than steel, and sharper than steel can be made, and tho' you throw it with more than Herculean force and precision, you shall no more be able to pierce him, than to penetrate the hard shell of a tortoise with a rye straw.[18]

5. Engagement and compassion for all people are central humanist values, aka the humanist argument

Humanists are concerned for the well being of all, are committed to diversity, and respect those of differing yet humane views.[19]

Prominent figures in the atheist movement talk frequently about how our society should recognize the contributions and worth of atheists, and how everyone should decry rhetorical attacks against the nonreligious. But this argument falls flat when some atheists fail to extend that claim to other communities – especially ones facing frequent rhetorical *and physical* attacks, such as the American Muslim and Sikh communities.

As a minority community in America's religious milieu, it makes strategic sense for atheists to ally with Muslims, Sikhs, and others. But as a *humanist* atheist, I feel a sense of moral obligation to stand up against identity-based hatred, no matter whom it's directed at. Not only is it absurd to hope that people should care about the lack of acceptance for atheists in the United States without also hoping that society will similarly embrace other communities, it's also selfish. Atheists who remain silent about systemic Islamophobia aren't just missing out on a strategic opportunity to highlight the parallels between their own experiences and those of other disenfranchised religious

18.   "Speeches and Letters of Abraham Lincoln, 1832–1865," Amazon.com: Kindle Store, http://www.amazon.com/, accessed March 30, 2011.
19.   "Humanist Manifesto III," American Humanist Association, 2003, http://www.americanhumanist.org/, accessed November 30, 2011.

minorities – they're opting out of an opportunity to do what is right, to take the moral high road, and to *demonstrate* what we keep telling the rest of the world: that atheists can be "good without God."

There's been a great deal of discussion in the atheist movement in recent years about social justice focused on anti-atheist bias, sexism, racism, homophobia and transphobia, ableism, and more.[20] These are, of course, crucial hurdles to overcome in the quest for human progress – but social justice should mean justice for *all*, including religious people. In fact, this is exactly what "social justice" *means*.

A study by Jeremy Stangroom may shed some light on why some atheists' definitions of social justice don't seem to include the religious. He found that 32 percent of atheist respondents felt that "they are not morally obliged to help somebody in severe need in India, even though to do so wouldn't cost them much, compared to only 22% of Christians who respond the same way (a difference that is easily statistically significant)." He continued:

> In other words, the data shows that people who self-identify as Christians are considerably more likely to think there is a moral obligation to help somebody in severe need (in India) than people who self-identify as atheists...

> A possible (partial) explanation for this failure, supported by the data noted above, is that many (online) atheists don't believe they have a strong moral obligation towards relatively anonymous or distant others, or don't feel the pull of such an obligation even if they believe they have it (or think they believe they have it).

Stangroom also noted another recent study that asked whether respondents would be willing to give a small donation to an overseas aid agency:

> The data shows that only 31% of people who self-identify as athe-ists respond that they are morally obliged to make such a donation, compared to 36% of people who self-identify as Christian, a differ-ence that is statistically significant... Moreover, if we also look at people who also self-identify as Muslim and Jewish (i.e., as adher-ents of Judaism), then the gap between how atheists and people who self-identify as religious respond widens (31% to 38%).[21]

20.   Jen McCreight, "Atheism+" *Blag Hag* blog, August 19, 2012, http://freethoughtblogs.com.

21.   Jeremy Stangroom, "Atheists, Morality and Distant Others," *Talking Phi-losophy: The Philosopher's Magazine Blog*, August 19, 2012, http://blog.talkingphilosophy.com.

I wonder if one of the issues at work is that some atheists see Muslims, Sikhs, and other religious individuals as distant others. There are female atheists, queer atheists, and atheists of all different races and ethnicities, so social justice for women, LGBTQ people, and racial and ethnic minorities is accessible – these issues impact many people in the atheist community. But what about people in other communities?

If this is the case, then interfaith outreach and cooperation is imperative as it strives to decrease the distance between "others" and create opportunities for people to identify shared values and a sense of shared humanity – an understanding of identity that allows people to see another's freedom and value as connected to their own.

II. Two Common Critiques

Since I started writing and speaking about interfaith work as a humanist, I've read a significant amount of criticism of nontheists participating in these efforts. From this writing it seems a large percentage of atheist interfaith opponents have kept their distance from interfaith work. I understand their hesitation, but I can't help wondering if there is some disconnect when those who most heavily criticize the interfaith movement also seem to have had little or no actual experience with it. I could be wrong, but I'd be surprised if someone who had been involved in interfaith work would suggest – as prominent atheist and widely recognized humanist PZ Myers, who was awarded Humanist of the Year by the American Humanist Association in 2009 and International Humanist in 2011 by the International Humanist and Ethical Union, did – that it "cheerfully and indiscriminately embrace[s] every faith without regard for content."[22]

Almost every argument I've read or heard from atheists opposed to interfaith work employs two critiques, and they're directly related: that interfaith leaves no room for religious criticism, and that it by default excludes atheists because atheism isn't a "faith." Atheists' rejection of interfaith work seems to be due in large part to an underlying assumption that, in order to participate, everyone must bite his or her tongue and play nice, and that participation in this kind of movement lends our implicit approval to "faith" as a concept and rallying point.

22.   PZ Myers, "What is This 'Interfaith' Nonsense, Anyway?" *Pharyngula*, March 19, 2011, http://scienceblogs.com/pharyngula/, accessed March 23, 2011.

Unsurprisingly, the idea that interfaith work requires significant tongue-biting makes many atheists very uncomfortable; it was certainly a concern I had before I started working in the interfaith movement. The irony of this worry is that the atheist and interfaith movements actually share a common point of origin: they both started, in part, as a reaction to religious extremism. Much like the atheist movement, the interfaith movement seeks to build inter-group understanding, encourage critical thinking, and end religiously based social and political exclusivism. The fundamental misunderstanding many people have is imagining that the interfaith movement is uninterested in combating religious totalitarianism and that it exists solely to maintain religious privilege – as an excuse to show that religion, in its many diverse forms, owns morality.

This concern couldn't be further from the truth. In fact, atheists participating in interfaith programs actually disrupt religious privilege by asserting that, for most of us, religious beliefs have little or nothing to do with our ethics. But if atheists do not participate in ongoing interfaith efforts, we leave the field open for the idea that faith is the only driving factor that compels people to work for a better world. By opting not to participate, atheists leave the ground uncontested for people of faith to claim. But by showing up, atheists demonstrate that religion does not have a monopoly on morality.

In my experience, interfaith work exists to eliminate religious privilege by bringing diverse religious and nonreligious people into common work to build relationships that might deconstruct the kind of "us versus them" thinking that contributes to exclusivist religious hierarchy. It is a place to challenge and question, but to do so constructively. The success of such challenges is contingent on whether invested relationships exist between the involved parties. If not, disagreements run the risk of degenerating into shouting matches in place of reasonable discourse.

Whether engaging Christians around my negative experiences as a former evangelical and as a queer person, or challenging my religious peers to explain their beliefs rationally, I've found interfaith work to not only be a fruitful place for such conversations but, in fact, the ideal forum for it. I can fondly recall any number of incidents when I argued theology and philosophy with religious colleagues while doing interfaith work and how, later, they told me that they actually took my perspective seriously because we had built a trusting relationship. It made all the difference that I treated them as intellectual equals – as people with respectable goals rather than just mindless adherents of some stupid religion. They had heard positions similar to mine in the past from other atheists, but the arguments had been presented so disrespectfully that they made no impact, and in some cases closed my religious colleagues to even entertaining such ideas.

This is precisely what interfaith work sets out to do: elicit civil dialogue to increase understanding, not stifle it for the sake of "playing nice."

There is a related concern many atheists have about joining interfaith coalitions: that participating in this work somehow bolsters religious privilege. And, all the more, that some people will conflate atheists participating in interfaith work with the idea that atheism is "just another religion," when some of the underlying values of a religious mindset are exactly what many atheists reject.

I can only speak from my experience here, but I have been clear in interfaith settings that I don't see my atheism and Humanism as religions. There remains disagreement among many about how to classify atheism and Humanism, and such disagreement often rises and falls on differing definitions of religion – but while there are a significant number of self-identified religious humanists, I find the distinction between atheism and the popular definition of the word religion is easy enough to maintain.[23]

I fully acknowledge that the language of "interfaith" is imperfect, clunky, and can feel exclusive to many nonreligious people. But I think we should participate in interfaith efforts anyway. Interfaith is currently the most recognized term to describe activities that bring the religious and nonreligious together for dialogue and common work; it is used far and wide by many, including the Obama administration. (When President Obama announced his Interfaith and Community Service Campus Challenge, he specifically highlighted the nonreligious as key stakeholders in this work.)[24]

I believe that change will come from within – that by participating in interfaith work, the nonreligious will broaden the meaning of such efforts and that the language used to describe them will change accordingly. This has certainly been true of my experiences in the interfaith movement – when I first began, the language was often quite religious-centric. But in just a few years, it has shifted dramatically to include the nonreligious. One example is an interfaith organization I have collaborated with in Massachusetts that

23.   The discussion around competing definitions of religion is beyond the scope of this essay, but certainly many Humanists – including some Ethical Culture members and other self-identified religious Humanists – consider non-supernatural experiences such as awe, wonder, and humility to be religious experiences. Others prefer to consider these experiences secular. I fall in the latter camp but it is a subject of debate and, I think, a discussion worth having. My thanks to Ethical Culture leader Hugh Taft-Morales and others who have engaged me in this discussion.

24.   "The President's Interfaith and Community Service Campus Challenge," Office of Faith-based and Neighborhood Partnerships, 2011, http://www.whitehouse.gov/.

fights homelessness. When I first began to work with them, they went by the name Social Action Ministries. Soon, however, we began a discussion about their name. Before long, they decided to change it to Social Action Massachusetts. In a guest post for my blog about this decision, their coordinator, Caitlin Golden, wrote:

> We don't want to be just inter*faith* – our dialogue and our action will only be truly inclusive if they also include the voices of those who do not identify with the *faith* part of interfaith at all. This isn't about 'watering down' the conversation to a lowest common denominator or pretending that we're all in theological or philosophical agreement, but rather about creating the space for people of diverse identities to share the values that lead them to engage in social action.[25]

To atheists concerned about being seen as "just another faith" and worried that interfaith isn't an avenue for substantive discourse: I encourage you to give it a shot anyway, and be vocal about where you stand. I cannot begin to recount all of the times interfaith work has opened up a space for robust conversations on problematic religious practices and beliefs. In fact, it has been a hallmark of my experience working in the interfaith movement. Furthermore, it has allowed me to engage religious people about atheist identity and eradicate significant misconceptions about what atheism is and what it isn't.

I regularly hear from atheists who are leading the charge for interfaith cooperation on their campuses and in their communities, and their experiences echo mine. They too have found that interfaith is expanding to incorporate them and that, when done well, interfaith engagement doesn't require that people check their convictions at the door; it invites people to try to understand and humanize the other.

It's a worthy goal – a necessary one – and if the only thing keeping some atheists from participating is a disagreement with the term "interfaith," then that is a missed opportunity.

III. Three Frequently Asked Questions

1. Why interfaith efforts?

A common question that rises from the above section is to question why we need *interfaith* efforts, specifically. Atheists work with believers every day

25.   Caitlin Golden, "Beyond Interfaith: Why We Changed our Name," July 14, 2011, *NonProphet Status*, http://nonprophetstatus.com/.

– at work, in school, when volunteering. So why are specifically interfaith events valuable?

Interfaith work is unique because it puts religious differences to the forefront. Nontheist participants can no longer be tokenized as the atheist neighbor who happens to be a good person; instead we show how our humanist beliefs inspire us to be good people. We demonstrate not only our shared values and a sense of common humanity, but we help legitimize atheists as a moral community in the context of cooperative work and values-based dialogue between other moral communities. And while I yearn for a more accurate label than "interfaith" to describe this work, I believe that the language of interfaith will evolve as more atheists get involved. What matters is that the work occurring in "interfaith" contexts aligns with humanist principles and goals – and it does.

2. What about religion?

A nontheist involved in interfaith efforts will have to grapple with what attitude he or she wants to take towards the religious beliefs of other participants. In that vein, it has been suggested that interfaith work asks nonbelievers to put their beliefs aside in order to get along.

I can't speak for all atheist interfaith activists, but this is not the case for me. The pursuit of truth matters. I believe that a naturalistic worldview that prioritizes scientific skepticism provides the best lens to consider our world. I have often relished debates about the legitimacy of religious claims, and I believe that ideas and words have consequences. Blind confidence in unsubstantiated beliefs can directly contribute to the problems our society faces. Well-reasoned conclusions, not faith-based dogma, ought to be the basis for public policy.

Still, I think it worth asking: When we advocate for something we think is true, what is our underlying goal? What kind of world are we working toward? Is there enough value in persuading believers out of religion if this change in their beliefs doesn't also change their approach to other important questions? It seems to me that I have more in common with someone who believes in God and who also values scientific progress and human rights than I do with an atheist who believes that women are inferior to men, or that not all people deserve equal access to education and health care.

Some have argued that the best way to fight injustice is by opposing religion, claiming that a world without religion would be a more just one. This idea neglects to account for the fact that religion has been cited as the source of both good and bad actions, and it's an overly simplistic assessment of a

complex issue. Basically good people do evil – or at least morally questionable – acts all the time, often without any religious influence at all.

Even for atrocities that seem to be religiously motivated, the data suggests
that people's motivations are complex. Research by social psychologists at
the New School for Social Research and the University of British Columbia
found that "prayer to God, an index of religious devotion, was unrelated to
support for suicide attacks." Instead, they found that attending religious services positively predicted support for suicide bombing – because it builds
coalitional commitment.[26] But this same phenomenon is present in more secular groups. For example, Sri Lanka's nonreligious, nationalistic Tamil Tigers
have used similar mechanisms to recruit support for suicide attack – and they
are responsible for more suicide bombings than any other group since the
1980s.[27]

Additionally, an important Pew Report interview with Robert A. Pape
challenges the supposed link between terrorism and religious extremism:
"What more than 95 percent of all suicide terrorist attacks since 1980 have
in common is not religion, but a specific secular goal: to compel modern
democracies to withdraw military forces from the territory the terrorists
view as their homeland."[28]

According to Dr Robert Pape, director of the Chicago Project on Suicide
Terrorism and author of *Dying to Win*,[29] where religious forces do become
most relevant is in demonizing the enemy and building out-group hostility, which supports the idea that humanizing religious diversity – one of
the primary goals of interfaith work – is vital. Thus, I am skeptical of the
claim that we should focus on bringing about an end to religion. Instead, we
should work with religious allies to directly tackle the very real problems
of dogmatism, authoritarianism, rigid tribalism, and social pressure – and
focus on promoting access to education.

26.   Jeremy Ginges, Ian Hansen and Ara Norenzayan, "Religion and Support for
       Suicide Attacks," *Psychological Science* 2.2, pp. 224–30, http://www.hecc.
       ubc.ca/files/2012/07/GingesHansenNorenzayan2009.pdf.
27.   "Tamil Tigers: Suicide Bombing Innovators," *NPR*, May 21, 2009, http://
       www.npr.org.
28.   "In God's Name? Evaluating the Links between Religious Extremism and
       Terrorism," *Pew Research Religion and Public Life Project*, October 21,
       2005, http://www.pewforum.org.
29.   Robert Pape, *Dying to Win: The Strategic Logic of Suicide Terrorism* (New
       York: Random House, 2006).

3. What about the truth?

In one discussion around *Faitheist*, a commentator suggested that eliminating ignorance is more important than eliminating injustice or suffering – and that if eliminating a particular ignorance resulted in greater suffering, it would still be a net positive. I cannot bring myself to agree with that. (Interestingly, I find this statement reminiscent of Mother Teresa's view that suffering was good if it brought people closer to God – for which the late Christopher Hitchens appropriately excoriated her.)

A commitment to knowledge is important, but it is not the *only* important commitment. In a world full of suffering that is frequently splintered by religious disagreements, I think humanists should sometimes prioritize the pursuit of justice over pursuing philosophical agreement – especially because hostile arguments over matters of truth frequently do little more than convince all involved of their own correctness. In the face of hostility, few people become more open; more often than not, we become defensive.

You can be honestly and strongly critical of religious beliefs and doctrines while acknowledging each individual's right to his or her personal beliefs, even if they seem irrational to you. To quote Christopher Hitchens: "I propose a pact with the faithful… as long as you don't want your religion taught to my children in school, given a government subsidy, imposed on me by violence, any of these things, you are fine by me."[30] This kind of attitude creates space for atheist-religious cooperation on important matters like secularism, education, and scientific and social progress, while also allowing everyone to be honest about their disagreements. I'm more concerned about whether someone shares most of my core values – such as pluralism, freedom of conscience, social cooperation, compassion, education – than whether they are religious or not. Many religious believers are at the forefront of efforts to promote human flourishing, and those shared concerns are more important to me than the fact that we don't agree about the existence of any gods.

We shouldn't de-emphasize concerns about truth, but while we pursue truth together, we can work for justice now. While it's unlikely that we'll see a world without religious belief anytime soon, there are important issues of human suffering that we can work to resolve right now. As a humanist, I find it extremely unlikely that a divine or supernatural force will intervene in human affairs to alleviate suffering. It is up to us human beings. By

---

30.   Christopher Hitchens and Tony Blair, *Hitchens vs. Blair: Be It Resolved Religion is a Force for Good in the World (The Munk Debates)* (Toronto: House of Anansi Press, 2011), p. 34.

working together – religious believers and unbelievers – we can accomplish a lot more. At the same time, we can work for the destigmatization of atheists, which will eventually contribute to the decrease of ignorance. We can encourage a more civil and open dialogue about faith and reason, helping people come to terms with prejudices that might prevent them from considering alternate views.

This conversation begins when humanists step out and share their stories with others, and listen to the stories of people outside the humanist community. Sociologist Marshall Ganz writes that, "stories are what enable us to communicate [our] values to one another."[31] Psychologist Dan P. McAdams elaborates on this idea, suggesting that the values we exemplify through story move into action and vision: "Narrative guides behavior in every moment, and frames not only how we see the past but how we see ourselves in the future."[32]

How will we guide our behavior, and who will we cooperate with in our actions to improve the conditions of life for others? What future will we imagine for ourselves and for the world? Is it a future in which the religious and secular will continuously come into conflict? One where religion is nothing more than a problem to be eradicated? In the words of Patel: will we make of religious differences a "bomb of destruction, a barrier of division"; or can we use our humanist values of reason in the service of compassion to build "a bridge of cooperation"?[33]

Perhaps we can, if we build relationships with our religious neighbors, listen to their stories, and act – together – on the shared values those stories communicate.

31.   Marshall Ganz, "Why Stories Matter," *Sojourners*, March 2009, www.sojo. net, accessed June 22, 2011.

32.   Benedict Carey, "This is your Life (and How You Tell It)," *New York Times*, May 22, 2007, http://www.nytimes.com, accessed June 19, 2010.

33.   Eboo Patel, "Religion Today: Bomb, Barrier or Bridge?" *Huffington Post*, August 5, 2010, http://www.huffingtonpost.com, accessed September 3, 2010.

Section II:

On Living, Celebrating, and Remembering Relationships

4 Forming Godless Community

Greg M. Epstein[*]

While I was researching and writing the chapter below – over several years leading up to the fall 2009 publication of my book *Good without God*, from which it is taken – the concept of humanist community was viewed very differently in the United States.[1] Most American humanist organizations were primarily focused on political and academic work. Community-building did not seem to me to be a major emphasis of the US secular movement, to the extent that such a movement even existed. I saw myself, at that time, as a young author who had been studying the history of world religions for years, and who wanted to help make an important case that in the twenty-first century, my fellow nontheistic and nonreligious people had a lot to learn about the practice of religion. Not that we needed to *be* religious, or that we needed to adopt any specific religious practice, or that we needed to stop criticizing religious wrongs. But if we wanted to build a humanist movement that would be a viable, sustainable, influential part of twenty-first century culture,

* Greg M. Epstein serves as the Humanist Chaplain at Harvard University, and is author of the New York Times bestselling book, *Good without God: What a Billion Nonreligious People Do Believe*. He currently serves as Vice President of the 36-member corps Harvard Chaplains. In 2005 Greg received ordination as a Humanist Rabbi from the International Institute for Secular Humanistic Judaism, where he studied in Jerusalem and Michigan for five years. He holds a BA (Religion and Chinese) and an MA (Judaic Studies) from the University of Michigan, Ann Arbor, and a Masters of Theological Studies from the Harvard Divinity School. Greg's work has been featured by the *New York Times*; CBS News; ABC World News with Diane Sawyer; ABC News Network; Al Jazeera; Fresh Air with Terry Gross, and numerous other programs on National Public Radio; BBC Radio; *USA Today*; *Newsweek*; *US News and World Report*; *The Boston Globe*, and many more.

1. "Good without God in Community: The Heart of Humanism," in Greg M. Epstein, *Good without God: What a Billion Nonreligious People Do Believe* (New York: William Morrow Paperbacks, 2010), ch. 6. *Good.* Many thanks to my editor David Highfill and everyone at HarperCollins Publishers for granting permission to use the material here.

then we were going to have to take the best ideas in religious community-building, and put them to work for us – and for humanity – in a secular context. The question was, would anyone listen or agree?

As I write these introductory words in 2014, humanists, atheists, and nonreligious people are creating a renaissance of community-building activity, in the United States and around the world. "Godless congregations" are popping up like popcorn in a microwave. Hundreds of thousands of people are joining atheist and humanist meet-up groups. But for the vast majority of such people a major question still remains: what should we do when we get together? And many more millions of nonreligious people who *might* find it interesting and worthwhile to get involved in building humanist community have not yet done so, for a variety of reasons. The discussion below is offered at this stage to answer lingering questions, and to remind us to be aware of our history and pursue excellence. Now more than ever, humanist community, if done well, has the power to change the world.

Humanism and atheism often lose out to religion not because of anything remotely related to theological belief, or even because people need to think of themselves as *better* than others, but we often cannot help but think of ourselves as part of a valued particular group and that group is often associated with religion. Whenever this starts sounding too theoretical to me, I think back to an old friend of mixed white Protestant background who, when I was wavering about whether I wanted to become a humanist rabbi because I wasn't sure how big a deal I wanted to make out of my own Jewish heritage, said enviously, "you're so lucky to have a *culture* – I'm *nothing!*"

Atheist Anglicans, Cultural Catholics, and Other True Christians

As I am humanist by faith, a Jew by cultural heritage, and a humanist chaplain and rabbi by profession, you might think that I am commenting on Christianity as something of an outsider.

Not necessarily so. I am also an American, and while I repudiate the notion that this country was founded on or is beholden to Christian principles, I have been influenced – usually for good – almost everywhere I've been across the country, by America's profoundly Christian *culture*. Like the billions of people around the world who watch our elections with profound interest because their fate will be affected by the outcome regardless of where they live, I have always watched American Christian culture with the deep curiosity of one whose life will be shaped by its twists and turns.

Of course, the obvious questions will be: Is Christianity a culture or just a belief? If one ceases to believe in Christian dogma, does one not cease to be a Christian? Never mind that even Bertrand Russell, in his famous essay "Why I am Not a Christian," allowed that he *was* a Christian in a demographic or cultural sense.[2] I had a fascinating conversation on this topic last year at the Shrove Tuesday Pancake Supper at Harvard's Memorial Church. After eating my fill of delicious blueberry pancakes traditionally offered as a treat before the austerity of Lent, I joined the church choir director and several students in standing around a piano and singing "Que Sera Sera," and then talked to my friend the Reverend Jon Page, a charismatic, young, liberal Protestant minister about the cultural differences among Christians. To Jon, a religious history major at Harvard and a graduate of Yale Divinity School, it is obvious that Christianity is as often a culture as a religion – you can see it not only because of the kinds of traditions represented by our dinner itself, but also in the clear sociological differences that separate American Protestant groups much more than does theology: Baptists tend to be poorer; Methodists more middle class; Presbyterians wealthier; Congregationalists tend to trace their roots directly back to English Puritans; one could go on.

No less than Richard Dawkins has called himself a Cultural Christian, along with many other prominent atheists such as the writer Sarah Vowell, who notes that her Pentecostal upbringing affected her deeply, as did her reading of the Bible (a "book club where they actually read the book") and talks about Martin Luther King Day as a holiday for secular Christians.

Unitarian Universalism

The "liberal religion" of Unitarian Universalism (UU) at times functions as a kind of humanist Christianity in practice – many UUs are humanists and many humanists are involved in UU. Unitarian Universalism formed in 1961 through a merger of two very liberal Christian denominations, the Unitarians and the Universalists. Some of those who orchestrated the merger, particularly among the Unitarians, were hoping the new Unitarian Universalist Association (UUA) would become the nation's first movement of humanist congregations. That isn't quite how things worked out – Unitarian Universalism has described itself since its inception as a religion without a creed, and thus open to both theists and humanists of a number of varieties – as long as they self-identify with Unitarian Universalism and its liberal tenets such

2.   Bertrand Russell, *Why I Am Not a Christian and Other Essays on Religion and Related Subjects* (New York: Touchstone, 1967).

as gender-egalitarianism, non-racism and non-ethnocentrism. Thus if you go to several of the 1100-plus UU Congregations across the US, what you will find there will vary tremendously from community to community. Some will simply be liberal churches. Others will be humanist meeting houses. In others you'll find a mix of practices with a heavy emphasis on Buddhism or Paganism.

Former UUA President and historian of Religious Humanism William F. Schulz has written of his "guilt" that Unitarian Universalism itself is one reason humanists have not had more success building their own unified movement. Schulz argues the original Religious Humanists, despite their allegiances to Unitarian and Universalist groups, intended to build their own independently organized movement of congregations, but ultimately came to rely on the UUA's congregations, where they have lost their voice among other more theological groups. Even if nearly half of the 200,000 Unitarian Universalists are self-professed humanists, as opposed to what has generally been the American Humanist Association's smaller size, Schulz admits that those humanists no longer feel as comfortable in a movement that in recent years has been dominated by a more theistic leadership and general character. When I recently attended one of the UUA's impressive national gatherings, I was struck by the two opposing narratives I heard regarding the presence of humanists and atheists in the movement. On the one hand, I heard a story about a humanist who stood up at a large conference Q&A session, and vented his frustration at what he saw as the excessive godliness of much current UU practice. At the end of his remarks he asked, "Are you going to miss us when we're gone?" On the other hand, there was the speaker's response: "Why can't you just let us have our metaphors?"

Black/African American Humanism

One of Unitarian Universalism's most difficult moments came in the late 1960s, when most of the Black delegates to the UUA unceremoniously cut their ties with the movement, over what they essentially saw as Unitarian Universalism's insufficient progressiveness with regards to Black leadership and its desire for separate Black UU institutions. This was a damning attack to level against a movement so eager to see itself as racially and otherwise universal, but it was also perhaps one of the strongest proofs that Unitarian Universalism embodies the culture of a particular demographic group – mainstream, liberal, highly educated white Judeo-Christian Americans.

American Blacks may be largely Christian, but despite having "religion" in common with many whites, they are obviously a cultural group unto themselves. Black American religious institutions exist not merely to promote Jesus' teachings, or Muhammad's for that matter. Rather, they play the crucial role that they do in their community because they provide it with a place of its own to congregate and celebrate itself and its history. The Black Church has played a unique role in Black American cultural life; for decades after slavery, it was the sole Black institution racism did not hinder; this generated an intense loyalty. As much as Blacks have valued integration, to suggest that they should become so Universalist as to give up the kinds of intra-community ties that the Black Church has come to represent would be an affront, not even a very humanistic thing to ask.

Granted, it is also the case that Black Americans have among the highest rates of professed belief in God of any American demographic group. Nevertheless, Anthony Pinn, a prolific writer and professor of Religion at Rice University, eloquently champions the concept of African American Humanism. Pinn's writings, such as *By These Hands: A Documentary History of African American Humanism*, and *African American Humanist Principles: Living and Thinking Like the Children of Nimrod*, achieve a rich demonstration that humanistic thought can be found across Black American history from the end of slavery – Fredrick Douglass, W. E. B. Du Bois, Zora Neale Hurston, and many others – through the Civil Rights Movement, whose ideological underpinnings, he argues, "were crystalized through their humanist posture toward communal action."[3] Pinn points out that A. Phillip Randolph, a truly great labor leader by any standard who was known as the "dean of Negro leaders" right up to the time Martin Luther King Jr stepped up to the national stage, was a committed humanist, even signing the American Humanist Association's Humanist Manifesto II in 1973.[4] And he illustrates the creative spirit of Black Humanism by selecting wonderfully freethinking passages from important African American literary works such as this excerpt from Richard Wright's canonical memoir *Black Boy*:

> One boy, who lived across the street, called on me one afternoon and his self-consciousness betrayed him; he spoke so naively and clumsily that I could see the bare bones of his holy plot and hear the creaking of the machinery of Granny's maneuvering.
>
> "Richard, do you know we are all worried about you?" he asked.

3.   Anthony B. Pinn, *African American Humanist Principles: Living and Thinking like the Children of Nimrod* (New York: Palgrave Macmillan, 2004), ch. 2.
4.   Anthony B. Pinn, *By These Hands: A Documentary History of African American Humanism* (New York: New York University Press, 2001); Pinn, *African American Humanist Principles*.

"Worried about me? Who's worried about me?" I asked in feigned surprise.

"All of us," he said, his eyes avoiding mine. "Why?" I asked.

"You're not saved," he said sadly.

"I'm all right," I said, laughing.

"Don't laugh, Richard. It's serious," he said.

"But I tell you that I'm all right."

"Say, Richard, I'd like to be a good friend of yours."

"I thought we were friends already," I said.

"I mean true brothers in Christ," he said.

"We know each other," I said in a soft voice tinged with irony.

"But not in Christ," he said.

"Friendship is friendship with me."

"But don't you want to save your soul?"

"I simply can't feel religion," I told him in lieu of telling him that I did not think I had the kind of soul he thought I had."[5]

The concept of "redemptive suffering" – that earthly suffering is desirable as an end unto itself, because it leads to redemption after death – is, for Pinn, the strongest reason to cut ties with the Black Church. He paints a painful picture of the harm it has done a Black community that has been subjected, and at times subjected itself, to so much intense and *unnecessary* suffering. We can only imagine what might have been if more American Blacks adopted the humanist stance that suffering is purposeless and to be struggled against, towards the goal of a more dignified life for all. Still, despite the solid intellectual and theoretical foundation Pinn lays out, he sees himself as a "humanist in search of a home." He does not have the congregational equivalent of a Black Church, but wants one; "Regarding this, I agree with Cornel West – institutional affiliation helps ground the intellectual's role in social transformation." Perhaps under an African American President who is also in search of a congregation, and who has written eloquently of his late

5.   Richard Wright, *Black Boy* (New York: Harper & Row, 1966), pp. 125–26.

mother's humanism, some progress can be made on this front in the coming years.[6]

Other Cultural Humanisms

Because the stream of goodness without God runs through every society and culture, the potential for a "cultural humanism" exists everywhere we might look. Amartya Sen, in *The Argumentative Indian* and *Identity and Violence* has sketched the outlines of an Indian identity thoroughly informed and inspired by humanism from the Carvaka and Lokayata through modern times.[7] The Indian city of Vijayawada, Andrapradesh has had a very active Atheist Centre since the days of Gandhi, who was an admirer of its founder. The Atheist Centre has since those days sponsored a variety of programs combating social inequality and injustice, providing free education in science and the humanities to children of untouchables and other poor classes, and otherwise breaking the often oppressive hold that conservative Hindu traditions can have on rural, underprivileged Indians. Gandhi was in fact well aware that he occasionally lost volunteers in the region who had left his compound to go and work with the less famous Gora, the founder of the Atheist Centre, because Gora was doing more good than Gandhi for the untouchables! There are also organizations like Indicorps – a cultural and service organization for members of the Indian diaspora, started by social entrepreneur Anand Shah and his two siblings just after the millennium.

The Muslim apostate Ibn Warraq (a pen name taken by Islamic infidels over the years) has been prolific and increasingly known in recent years for his books and describing the process of turning to humanism from an Islamic perspective, and of attempting to bring about an "Enlightenment" in contemporary Islam by means of critical scholarship on the Quran, the history of intellectual and theological liberalism in Muslim circles, and on those who have "left Islam" as a dogmatic system of supernatural beliefs and accompanying rituals.

Tu Weiming, a scholar of Chinese history and philosophy and of Confucian studies, has devoted his internationally decorated career to making the case for Confucian Humanism: an affirmative, spiritual vision of Chinese and East Asian identity that makes an explicit commitment to universal Human Rights, ecological conservation, ecumenical dialogue, and

---

6.   Pinn, *African American Humanist Principles*, introduction.

7.   Amartya Sen, *The Argumentative Indian* (New York: Picador, 2005) and Sen, *Identity and Violence* (New York: W. W. Norton & Company, 2006).

progressive capitalism (or at least progressive anti-communism).[8] And noted French Buddhist scholar Stephen Batchelor makes a passionate plea for agnosticism and naturalism as not only an historical element of Buddhist philosophy but also an important aspect of contemporary Buddhism, in his recent bestselling work *Buddhism without Beliefs.*[9]

Humanistic Judaism

But if the theme here seems to be one of scholars and public intellectuals issuing erudite white papers about lofty ideas that never see the light of day-to-day practice, there is a reason to take heart.

Rabbi Sherwin Wine was a brilliant young reform rabbi in suburban Detroit when, in 1963, he rocked the American Jewish world by founding the first ever synagogue without God. He'd known he was a humanist nearly all his life, but loved the Jewish culture and community he grew up around, and loved the job of rabbi as held by the modern, liberal, elegantly dressed and groomed men who served his family in that capacity at their Conservative synagogue. The position of rabbi in affluent suburban Detroit around the War, after all, hardly revolved around offering devotions to God, studying obscure Talmudic texts, or henpecking Jews about following the laws of kashrut (how to keep kosher). All that crowd expected from its rabbi was a stately presence and some sagely wisdom when it came time to get married, hold a funeral, or bless a baby's coming into the world. The rabbi was expected to give an inspiring sermon, along the lines of a presidential speech, on the few times a year most Jews bothered to pass through the gilded old temple. He was supposed to set an example. And recite a few Hebrew prayers nobody paid much attention to anyhow.

It was a great gig, especially for a gifted showman like Sherwin, who loved people and loved to talk to them. Sherwin decided against a career in academia and instead became a Reform rabbi (and then a Jewish chaplain in the army serving in Korea) not in spite of his atheism, but in fact because Reform Judaism was the most liberal form of Jewish community in America back then. Many Reform rabbis were atheists, though they followed a kind of don't-ask, don't-tell policy about it with their congregations.

8.   See for example, Tu Weiming, "The Ecological Turn in New Confucian Humanism: Implications for China and the World," in Tu Weiming and Mary Evelyn Tucker, *Confucian Spirituality, Volume Two* (New York: The Crossroad Publishing Company, 2004).

9.   Stephen Batchelor, *Buddhism without Beliefs* (New York: Riverhead Trade, 1998).

But Sherwin refused to accept don't-ask-don't-tell-you-don't-believe. He wanted to say it out loud. And not just, "There is no God." More importantly, he had no stomach to waste time in front of his congregation, mouthing words no one took seriously ("Blessed art thou, o lord our God, ruler of the universe, who sanctified us with his commandments...") when he could be talking to them about things that really mattered: what does it mean to live a good life? What do we believe in, if not God? How do we cope with death, tragedy, and the absurd unfairness of life? How can we find the strength to be happy in the face of all the unhappiness around us?

So Sherwin gathered a group of people who were dissatisfied with the congregational options currently at their disposal, and told them he intended to do something new and different. He wanted to leave his synagogue behind and start a new one, meant to function as a community center for people, not a house of God. He recognized that Judaism is a culture, and can claim famous doubters from Freud to Woody Allen to Theodore Herzl, not to mention the 49 percent of American Jews today who say they are not Jewish by religion. Wine preached powerfully that we might take pride in our culture, while affirming the equality of all human beings as part of a humanist worldview. In this new synagogue, the philosophy, the message, and the driving force would not be Jewish theology, nor would it be any god at all. The congregation would focus on meeting human needs, especially the need to strive together for human dignity. Eight couples went with him to Birmingham, Michigan and formed something called the Birmingham Temple. Before long, *Time* magazine was decrying the "atheist rabbi" in Detroit.

When I met Sherwin Wine it was more than 35 years later. The Birmingham Temple had moved to nearby Farmington Hills, where it had grown to become a gorgeous, sprawling suburban synagogue for several hundred rebel Jews and their friends. The movement of Humanistic Judaism had taken root and spread to congregations and communities around the world. Sherwin had written several books such as the classic *Judaism beyond God*; founded a humanistic Jewish rabbinic program to train future humanist leaders; and publicly debated religious fundamentalists such as Jerry Falwell and Meir Kahane.[10] By that point he'd also performed thousands of weddings, funerals, bar and bat mitzvahs, and baby-naming ceremonies based not on praise of god but on celebration of the human spirit. And he'd listened at the bedside of hundreds of sick and dying patients with the same passion, commitment and warmth that drove him to found several humanist umbrella organizations nationally and internationally.

10.   Sherwin Wine, *Judaism beyond God* (New York: Society for Humanistic Judaism, 1985).

He listened to me, too. Back then I was still a confused post-adolescent, still exploring Buddhism and rock music. My father's death haunted me and my life choices expressed a subconscious whine, "Why me?" Without the theatrics of grabbing me by the collar, he patiently argued that life isn't fair, and the good life is not one of constant sensual pleasure or of narcissistic self-regard. Today I am among those dedicating our lives to carrying on the new humanistic tradition he helped weave into the older Jewish cultural tradition we are still connected to. As he described it:

> While many institutions in the old authoritarian religion were harmful, not all of them were. Congregations and rabbis were useful inventions. Secular Jews need full-service communities, and they need trained leaders who can respond not only to their Jewish cultural needs but especially to their human needs for coping with the human condition. Suffering and death are also Jewish. Struggling for happiness is also Jewish. In many ways humanistic congregations function in the lives of their members in the same way as Reform, Conservative, and Reconstructionist synagogues do. They provide the same services, ask the same questions – even though they provide different answers.[11]

Of course, from a humanistic perspective there is no reason to see even our most beloved heroes as perfect saints. Surely the movement he built is nowhere near as far along in its development today as it could be. There is a lot of work left to be done for those willing to do it. Moreover, he didn't get much of a chance to work on his belief that the combined forces of humanism and a cultural community could well serve many non-Jewish communities as well. I hope in the coming years we will see more actively organized groups of African American Humanists, Humanist Quakers and Unitarian Universalists, Indian Humanists, Humanist Buddhists, and the like. In any case, we will have a great model for such communities available to us, if we are willing to reach beyond ourselves and acknowledge our individual needs to come together with others and serve a higher human purpose.

Community

It seems almost everyone who's ever written about society, not to mention sociology, has an opinion on community – what it is, how and why we lost it, who took it from us, how we must get it back. From the Greeks who

11.   Sherwin Wine, "Reflections," in *A Life of Courage* (New York: International Institute for Secular Humanistic Judaism, 2004), pp. 291–92.

defined it as the inclusive state, but excluded anyone and everyone who got in the way of their ideal polis, to Augustine's argument that what we needed was a city of God, not a city of man, to Hegel's complaint that modernity was destroying our community, to Weber's analysis of *communitas* as belonging, and Durkheim's diagnosis of modern society's need for a new, post-traditional form of that belonging, all the way to the hot windstorm of today's discourse on community that is everyone from Rush Limbaughian whining that you can blame it all on the Democrats, to *Bowling Alone,* to deconstructionists and queer theorists who want to blow up yesterday's notions of community and start over again, and everywhere in between. It would be cruelly boring if I went through the history of all this just to make a point that can be put more succinctly. Here it is: community can be many things at any time for anyone. But whatever it is, we all know we need it. We all must have it.

An Ethical Culture

This chapter wouldn't be complete without the description of an important historic episode – the story of a man named Felix Adler and the movement of Ethical Culture he founded in 1876.

Adler was born in Germany in 1851 to a Reform rabbi father who immigrated to the United States when Felix was a boy, to become the rabbi of the wealthiest and most prestigious synagogue in New York City. Felix was something of a prodigy and given every opportunity at education, including being sent to Germany for rabbinical training of his own, where he internalized the momentous changes taking place in science and around the world, and thus decided that the Reform rabbinate could contain neither his philosophy nor his ambition.

In Germany, Adler decided to build a new religion that would be beyond science without being inconsistent with science. Upon his return home he began talking about it, and stirred enthusiasm in his peers. And in May 1876, not long after his 26th birthday, Adler took the stage in a rented hall to address his family, friends, and the collection of admirers and curious onlookers that had already begun to gather around him. Adler proposed a new movement meant to address a "great and crying evil in modern society. It is want of purpose." The new movement Adler proposed was intended "to entirely exclude prayer and every form of ritual…"[12] His address was gripping, inspiring, and full of humanistic conviction:

12.   Howard Radest, *Toward Common Ground* (New York: Unger, 1969), p. 27.

...freedom of thought is a sacred right of every individual man. Believe or disbelieve as you list – we shall at all times respect every honest conviction – but be one with us where there is nothing to divide – in action. Diversity in the creed, unanimity in the deed. This is that practical religion from which none dissents. This is that Platform broad enough to receive the worshipper and the infidel. This is that common ground where we may all grasp hands as brothers united in mankind's common cause...[13]

Adler took seriously his call for action and not words. A movement was incorporated almost immediately, and began to attract members rapidly. Meetings were set for each Sunday where Adler would deliver "Platform" addresses often outlining ideas for ambitious social service projects meant to correct the glaring injustices of the urban life of that time. He and his followers then got to work assembling those projects.

Within a few years Ethical Culture had created the first free-of-charge Visiting Nurses program in New York's history, to address the frightening tuberculosis epidemic of the 1880s. Young nurses from the Ethical community were sent into deathly city slums by themselves, or with their mothers if they were too young to go alone. The girls were taught that their mission was "to help others not for any future reward, but simply because we thought it was right to do right."[14] They must have made quite the sight for those young men, suffering in lonely beds – one of whom remarked he much preferred their visits to those of Catholic nuns "because we brought food to nourish his body while the Sisters were primarily interested in saving his soul."[15] Through the success of Ethical member Lillian Wald, this program was permanently incorporated into the city's network of social services and still does great good today – though, as planned by Adler and others in those days, Ethical Culture asked for and was given neither credit nor farther say in the fate of the charity it founded.

A beautiful building was erected on Central Park in 1910 that still stands, the size of a mega-church, as the home of the New York Society for Ethical Culture and its national body national American Ethical Union. The building was filled with a superstar cast of congregants and collaborators, including Jane Addams, Lillian Wald, Booker T. Washington, W. E. B DuBois, William James, Walt Whitman, and Samuel Gompers. Ethical Culture was also involved in the establishment of the National Association for the Advancement of Colored People in 1909, and Adler's successor as head of

13.   Radest, *Toward Common Ground*, p. 28.
14.   Radest, *Toward Common Ground*, p. 27.
15.   Radest, *Toward Common Ground*, p. 38.

the movement, John Lovejoy Elliot, was a key player in the founding of the American Civil Liberties Union or ACLU.

Unmistakably, Adler was a brilliant organizer who knew how to motivate and convince the most talented leaders of his day about the importance and worth of his mission. He also identified strong leaders who had impressive successes of their own – Stanton Coit, sent to London to begin to develop Ethical Culture overseas, set up an Ethical Church that made more effective use of symbols, ritual and music than what had thus far been developed in New York. Within several years of his arrival in England 600 people were regularly attending his weekly Sunday services.

Another successful project was the free kindergarten Adler and his colleagues founded to offer ethics, science, and soup to the city's poorest children. School organizers, including Adler, would knock on doors in the "gas house" district around 42nd Street with leaflets and idealism. Parents initially suspected it was some sort of elaborate kidnapping scheme. Unfortunately, the several schools Ethical Culture ultimately founded met the same fate as the Visiting Nurse program – after achieving great success, its founders turned their work over to the general public, taking little or no credit for themselves, for Ethical Culture, or for humanism.

According to Ethical Culture movement historian Howard Radest, these early efforts at social service also set a pattern in response to social need. A project for meeting that need would be devised and implemented, and thereafter move toward independence and ultimate lack of identification with Ethical Culture. Perhaps the austerity of Adler's ethic was a disservice to the movement he sought to build, for it guaranteed that much of the wealth, energy, and competence that rallied to Ethical Culture would be put at the disposal of causes outside of the movement itself.[16] The nomenclature issue reared its head as well: when, later in his life, his movement's next generation began to gravitate towards affiliation with the term humanism and its new organizations, Adler let pride and the narcissism of minor difference cloud his cooperative spirit, shunning the term humanism for what he described as its emphasis on "human ends" rather than "transcendental ideals" – even though he surely knew enough about the humanist movement at that time to know that its ideals were no more or less "transcendental" than his own.

Sadly, the Ethical community still has not really addressed the nomenclature issue – the divisions between it and humanism today are so minimal that the fact that some small community humanist and Ethical Culture groups don't significantly collaborate or even merge simply because of their different origins and names is tragicomic. And the movement hasn't

16.   Radest, *Toward Common Ground*, p. 40.

significantly revitalized its meeting format in 135 years – no religious denomination could ever survive that; and it hasn't changed the awkward name "Leader" for its clergy. Still, when compared to the beauty and pioneering relevance of Adler's vision for a congregation that could do great good without God, these concerns are minor. They can be fixed relatively easily with the will of current membership and an infusion of new interest.

The Ethical Culture building still stands as a living monument – the largest humanist congregational gathering house ever built. But more than that, it is a symbol of all the wonderful things humanists and the non-religious have done together in the past and can do even more of in the future: articulate scientifically sound and creatively inspiring values; build supportive and loving communities around those values; develop aesthetically powerful rituals and a sense of engagement with culture; serve the community with uncommon bravery and measurable success; and play a leading role in the most urgent social struggles of the age. For all that and more, the New York Center for Ethical Culture should be a place of pilgrimage: among a handful of must-see American tourist stops for anyone interested in humanism, atheism, secularism, or world religion generally – along with the Birmingham Temple in Michigan; the Center for Inquiry in Amherst New York; and the United States Congress (not because Jerry Falwell was right about it being a House of 600 humanists, but because any American humanist can arrange to visit his Congressional representative alongside the staff of the Secular Coalition for America, a dynamic group affiliated with organizations such as the American Humanist Association, the American Ethical Union, the Society for Humanistic Judaism, and many more).

Though at the time of this writing, the New York building has some chipping paint, it can still be a huge home for humanism. What will we do with it? And will we build more such centers in Boston? San Francisco? Atlanta? Austin? Buenos Aires, Barcelona, Beijing, Mumbai? Yes, we humanists also need to build more actual structures of our own. Only a tiny number of atheist and humanist groups and communities have their own buildings – but can you imagine a US Supreme Court session in some rented elementary school classroom, with justices sitting around on those little orange plastic chairs? We never really have a chance to build up the political, charitable, educational, or social work we do because we don't have our own spaces. Finding humanist congregation is not some oddball curiosity of an idea; it's not even a luxury, to be addressed after we succeed in getting "In God We Trust" off the dollar bill. If we ever want to be anything more than a downtrodden minority, it is a necessary response to one of our most aching and eternal human needs.

Now I fear I have pushed my allies more than some will want to tolerate. The world of organized humanism is as diverse as that of organized

Christianity or Judaism. It contains many viewpoints on what the non-religious ought to stand for and do. Many will agree with me that we can be good without God but strongly disagree with one or another aspect of my vision for humanist community. But I have the highest respect for and identification with those working in the various loosely connected streams of the humanist, atheist, Ethical, secularist and Freethought movement today. Their aims, for the very large part, are my aims. Their failures are my failures. And I dearly hope that if I am in any way successful as an individual, it will be because I have contributed to their success. I ask their forgiveness and understanding that it is simply not a humanist value to suspend one's judgment of history or reality in order to prop up one's friends with hagiography.

For all its flaws and foibles the entire movement has actually accomplished an incredible amount given that it has existed in an organized sense for, essentially, a single century. Given humanism's mobilization of ideas and recruiting of intellectual leadership, along with its strong influence on its religious contemporaries worldwide, it is fair to say that no spiritual movement worldwide has accomplished more in its first hundred years. And so it is my aim now to provoke serious thought, not only among religious people as to whether they have given the good without a god a fair shake, or also non-religious people about whether they might do better to affiliate with a movement that represents their ideals and needs their help, but even among active humanist leaders who are doing what I believe to be heroic work and will not be served by complacency, especially when they stand at the threshold of making a deep and visible difference in the world.

Osama Bin Laden's greatest success was in recognizing a generation ago that inequality, disenfranchisement and anger were where his part of the world was headed, and setting out to organize disaffected young men into a mass movement. As interfaith organizer Eboo Patel notes, when Bin Laden met Khalid Muhammad, Zarqawi, or Atta, he saw their entrepreneurial leadership skills first. He saw their potential as lieutenants, their ability to mobilize masses of young people to make his vision of radical Islam a reality. Eventually we will either match this combination of passion and pragmatism, or be overwhelmed by it.

Herding Cats, or "Community Organizing"

For too long, organized secularism has been an oxymoron, like herding cats. People who believed in a more humane, humanistic world mostly wrote off the possibility of gathering their peers together so that together they could actually have some influence. Weekly meetings were too dogmatic. Trained leaders were too priestly. Dedicated meeting spaces too churchy. Fundraising too smarmy and reminiscent of the worst evils of the collection plate – never mind that the very existence of cherished secular institutions like museums, universities, and the like depends on trained leadership, dedicated spaces, and fundraising.

But it would be one thing if the allergy was to top-down institutions alone. Bottom-up approaches to promoting goodness without God have been politely ignored. Many local and national secular communities will have the same president for decades. They do not have regular elections. They employ no outreach strategy with a prayer of ensuring many people beyond their insular social circles will ever hear of the group.

If all we stand for is, on the one hand, repudiating top-down religious authority as represented by the clergy, and on the other hand, with noses turned up, condescending towards more democratic, grass-roots efforts to organize humanist communities, and anything that reminds anyone in any way of a church is rejected – then that is not just cutting off our nose to spite our face, it's chopping off our head to spite our body.

But wherever there are good people, there are people who believe in being good without God. There are freethinkers wherever there are free people who are able to think. There are humanists wherever there are human beings.

The Obama campaign swept the United States in 2008 with the help of strategies and techniques that seemed radically new to everyone except those who actually knew what a "community organizer" actually does. Community organizing is nothing more, or less, than herding cats. It is offering people the opportunity to come together not out of ignorance, or because they are sheep, but because they are intelligent enough to understand that in a world without supernatural or natural miracles, only we can make the world a better place, and we simply cannot do it alone. Here is a letter to you, inspired by one of the many messages the Obama campaign sent over the course of its run to the Presidency – a run that was unexpected by most, but not too hard to understand for those of us who have studied community organizing and know its power:

Anyone in the world reading this has the potential to help build humanism – not just for our own sake or the sake of the individual humanist communities we will build and strengthen, but as a way of maximizing the impact that each of us as individuals can have on the entire world.

Now, after reading this chapter it's time to start sharing your ideas and energy with others that need them. It's time to seek out people from diverse backgrounds and experiences who, like you, are passionately committed to living a good life and building a good society, and who just happen to be among the millions who can soberly face the reality that this work must be done without God.

That's why I am asking you now, whether in conjunction with a local humanist, atheist, or secular group, or on your own initiative if no such group exists near you, to organize a meeting about humanism in your home, or elsewhere in your neighborhood.

Around the United States and the entire world, people like you who are committed to goodness without god or traditional religion, whether longtime humanist leaders or newcomers exploring these ideas, can host house meetings explicitly extending a hand to others who see themselves as humanists, atheists, agnostics, nonreligious, and so on – whether they've been involved in humanism before or are have never heard of it before.

The purpose of these meetings is to meet, get to know one another by sharing the stories of why you've chosen to embrace a human-centered philosophy of life, and then, based on the shared values that emerge from these diverse stories, build a grass-roots organization that can spread word (clean up parks, work for the environment, defend Church-State separation alongside progressive religious allies, celebrate holidays, weddings, and funerals, eventually move into buildings, and more) about humanism around your community. Together, groups like this around the globe can build community connections while fighting climbing change; defending Church-State separation alongside progressive religious allies; celebrating holidays, weddings, and funerals; and eventually acquiring their own physical centers that will be able to house community service programs like homeless empowerment and addiction recovery treatment driven by the best practices and latest scientific knowledge of our time; all while spreading religious freedom by allowing each person to decide for him or herself whether to embrace a humanistic or theistic worldview.

Sure, it's an ambitious project, and requires some commitment. But it's incredibly exciting to be involved, alongside your friends and neighbors, in a project that has global significance for a cause you care deeply about.

5   A Guide to Resources for Educating the Next Generation

Bob Bhaerman*

When Joss Whedon, the award-winning TV and movie writer and director, accepted the Outstanding Lifetime Achievement Award in Cultural Humanism at Harvard University in 2009, he stated that "the enemy of humanism is not faith; the enemy of humanism is hate, is fear, is ignorance." Whedon went on to declare that education "is categorically the one thing that we must bring to our neighborhoods, our people, our families, our world, [and] other countries." "Education, education, education," he repeated.[1] I agree: education is key, and providing children within a humanistic life perspective is vital.

For the past four-plus years, I have served as the director of the American Humanist Association's Kochhar Humanist Education Center. Having grappled with humanist education matters, I am pleased to share my perspectives and, particularly, some of the major resources that can be readily used by parents and teachers in bringing a humanist education to our neighborhoods, our people, our families, and around the world and thus meet our obligations to the next generation of humanists.

In my assessment we have a number of educational obligations to the next generation – our children and their children. The primary and overriding one is to *inoculate* (*not indoctrinate*) them against what I see as the ten modern-day plagues: dogmatism, self-delusion, brainwashing, closed-mindedness, intolerance, xenophobia, injustice, apathy, acceptance of antiquated myths, and religious absurdities. I am suggesting that we can do this in three ways: through education, action, and community building. What I provide here isn't a full essay outlining and analyzing various strategies as presented in the secondary literature of the Academy. Instead, consider what I offer below as an annotated bibliography of source materials for those seeking, a sketch of resources for education in light of humanism.

---

1. There are several places where Joss Whedon's talk can be heard, e.g., Joss Whedon on The True Enemy of Humanism | Mockingbird www.mbird.com/2009/04/joss-whedon-on-humanism-and-its-enemy/.

The Obligation to Teach Critical Thinking

The obligation to teach critical thinking appears at the top of nearly every educator's "Must Do" list and should be on top of every humanist educator's list as well. It surely was for Steven Schafersman, geologist and current President of Texas Citizens for Science, when he wrote his 1998 essay, "Critical Thinking and its Relation to Science and Humanism." Schafersman maintained that a person who thinks critically asks appropriate questions, gathers relevant information, sorts through this information efficiently and creatively, reasons logically from this information, and comes to reliable and trustworthy conclusions about the world. He listed 24 components of critical thinking beginning with focusing on problems and questions and ending with anticipating the consequences of one's actions. He then presented an extensive list of critical and uncritical thinking areas in which he compared logical and illogical thinking, pragmatic and wishful thinking, skeptical and authoritarian thinking, reflective and dogmatic thinking, realistic and idealistic thinking, creative and close-minded thinking, comprehensible and mystical thinking, and reasonable and emotional thinking. He concluded by stating that critical thinking is scientific thinking applied to questions and problems of everyday life.[2]

In light of Schafersman's framing of critical thinking, we are not at a loss in identifying good teaching resources in this area since many organizations have developed them. Here is a brief sampler of some of these organizations followed by some of their key resources:

- The Center for Critical Thinking and Moral Critique and the Foundation for Critical Thinking work to promote the cultivation of critical thinking. Their goal is to integrate research and theory and develop resources to help educators improve their instruction. The resources they offer include books, thinker's guides and videos.[3]
- The International Center for the Assessment of Higher Order Thinking's goal is to help educators at all levels design ways to determine their success at teaching critical thinking skills. They have developed the International Critical Thinking Test that is available through the Foundation for Critical Thinking.[4]
- The National Council for Excellence in Critical Thinking's goal is to articulate, preserve, and foster intellectual standards in critical

2.   The essay is available at www.freeinquiry.com.
3.   www.criticalthinking.org/.
4.   www.criticalthinking.org/about/internationalCenter.shtml.

thinking research, scholarship, and instruction. The Council is a creation of the Foundation for Critical Thinking.[5]

- The Philosopher's Club helps young people nurture "the fourth R," the ability to reason in constructive ways. Students are required to back up their views with compelling evidence in well-structured arguments. The Philosopher's Club is a project of the Society for Philosophical Inquiry that also has developed resources for adults.[6]

- The Teacher's Press is directed by Brant Abrahamson, an active member of the Humanists of West Suburban Chicagoland, who has prepared valuable resources for high school students on many topics. He and Fred Smith wrote *Thinking Logically: A Study of Common Fallacies,* a student text and two teacher's manuals that are excellent starting points for teaching critical thinking.[7]

- Foundation for Critical Thinking offers resources including text such as *Critical Thinking: How to Prepare Students for a Rapidly Changing World*; *Critical Thinking Handbook: K-3*; *Learning to Think Things Through: A Guide to Critical Thinking in the Curriculum*; and *Teacher's Handbook for Critical Thinking for Children*. The latter is designed for use in conjunction with *The Miniature Guide to Critical Thinking for Children*. Another valuable resource is *The Miniature Guide to Critical Thinking: Concepts and Tools* by Richard Paul and Linda Elder. The topics include The Elements of Thought, A Checklist for Reasoning, Three Levels of Thought, Three Kinds of Questions, What Critical Thinkers Routinely Do, Stages of Critical Thinking Development, and much more.[8]

Any of these resources above could be used in combination with the "*Teacher's Manual*" associated with Linda Elder's *The Miniature Guide to Critical Thinking for Children*.[9] The five components discussed in Elder's work are: Understanding Fictional Characters That Help Children Understand Critical Thinking; Introducing Fair and Unfair Thinking; The Intellectual Standards (i.e., helping children evaluate thinking, clarity, accuracy, relevance, logic and fairness); The Parts of Thinking; and The Intellectual Virtues. The manual includes "Thinking for Yourself Activities for Children."

5.   http://www.criticalthinking.org/about/nationalCouncil.shtml.
6.   www.philosopher.org/.
7.   www.freeinquiry.com/critical-thinking.html.
8.   www.criticalthinking.org/about/nationalCouncil.shtml.
9.   Linda Elder, *Critical Thinking for Children* (Tomales, CA: Foundation for Critical Thinking, 2006).

Humanist educators, I believe, are obligated to teach critical thinking along with humanist values of compassion, empathy, justice, kindness and caring. Critical thinking alone, however, is one of several essential skills discussed next.

An Obligation to Teach Essential Skill Areas

In the article on "A Vision of Humanist Education for our Complex World," Carol Wintermute, co-dean of The Humanist Institute, cites the work of Soraj Hongladarom, Director of the Center for Ethics of Science and Technology in Thailand. Hongladarom outlined four essential skill areas which must be provided for in "humanist education for tomorrow's world" including critical thinking. The four are communication, critical thinking, visualization and adaptability. Hongladarom – and Wintermute – stress that we need these four skills to cope with the unpredictable and complex problems we will encounter and that a humanist education must provide these abilities.[10] They are:

- Communication skills involve forming and presenting ideas clearly and precisely so that others understand the speakers' or writers' beliefs. In a world where new information is disseminated daily, those who deliver clear messages will be the ones most often heard. Humanist education, therefore, must emphasize that clear thought is only possible through clear language and that this skill is essential for coping with our changing world.
- Critical thinking skills are needed to sort through this mass of information to decide what is important and useful. This means suspending belief in some proposal or conclusion until proper evidence has been provided. "Critical thinking," Wintermute states, "is needed to keep us afloat in the waves of truth claims coming to our shores." I believe it is never too early – or too late – to teach the next generation how to swim!
- Visualization is the ability to imagine new solutions for old problems as well as to come up with fresh ideas. In our ever-changing world, those who can visualize the future can come up with creative solutions and see new directions in which to turn. "Individual independence," Wintermute maintains, "is predicated on being able

10.   The article can be found in *Essays in the Philosophy of Humanism* 18.1 (Spring-Summer, 2010), pp. 71–80.

to visualize what may come and to be prepared to deal with it in a creative and successful fashion."

- Adaptability is the ability to embrace change and face uncertainty with confidence. Living with ambiguity and the unpredictable is an essential coping skill for the future. Humanist education, therefore, must prepare the next generation to anticipate change, welcome it, and see it as inevitable and natural.

The Obligation to Teach Science Honestly and Accurately

The Discovery Institute's Center for Science and Culture has attacked the teaching of evolution and is scrambling the brains of children with such non-sense that the world was created, oh, about six thousand years ago. Fortunately, there are people and organizations leading the battle to teach science honestly and accurately. But it is an on-going battle.

To counter intelligent design and creationism, Eugenie Scott and Glenn Branch's *Not in our Classroom: Why Intelligent Design is Wrong in our Schools,* is the essential resource.[11] Scott is the Executive Director and Glenn Branch is the Deputy Director of the National Center for Science Education, the clearinghouse for information about protecting the teaching of science in public schools and especially the teaching of evolution. Barry Lynn of Americans United for Separation of Church and State writes in the book's foreword that "No matter how credible the scientific evidence is in the rest of this book; no matter how clear the constitutional arguments; no matter how well crafted the explanations that evolution and religious faith are not in conflict— this is not a battle that will go away soon." Another resource is Stanley Kramer's *How to Think like a Scientist: Answering Questions by the Scientific Method* written for children in grades 3 to 5.[12] After providing several points on how one can get the wrong answer to a question by not using all the available information, depending too much on other people's answers or wanting a certain result, Kramer presents situations that children are likely to run into in their daily lives.

Another valuable resource is "Thinking Like a Scientist," a science education program developed by Wendy Williams and her colleagues in the Department of Human Development at Cornell University. The program

11.   Eugenie Scott and Glenn Branch, *Not in our Classrooms: Why Intelligent Design is Wrong for our Schools* (Boston: Beacon Press, 2006).
12.   Stephen P. Kramer, *How to Think like a Scientist: Answering Questions by the Scientific Method* (New York: HarperCollins, 1987).

consists of 13 lessons that discuss the scientific method using issues and ideas relating to the lives of the average high school student.[13] The James Randi Educational Foundation also has excellent resources. Recently they developed an instructional module to allow high school students to come to their own conclusions about the validity of ESP claims through the use of carefully designed and controlled experiments. Students learn how to accurately evaluate the significance of the results guarding against experimenter error, bias, and intentional fraud.

The Skeptic's Society *provides many valuable insights that are not to be missed.* The Society is a scientific and educational organization of scholars, investigative journalists, historians, professors and teachers whose mission is to investigate and provide a sound scientific viewpoint on claims of the paranormal, pseudoscience, pathological science and, as they say, "plain old nonsense." Skepticism, they maintain, is the application of reason to any and all ideas. When they say "we are skeptical," they are simply stating that one must see compelling evidence before believing. The key to skepticism, they conclude, "is to continuously and vigorously apply the methods of science to navigate the treacherous straits between 'know nothing' skepticism and 'anything goes' credulity."[14] Carl Sagan once wrote that science is a way of thinking much more than it is a body of knowledge. He would, of course, have maintained that scientific thinking must be taught honestly and accurately.

Obligation to Bring Humanist Education to our Families

One of the best resources on bringing education to families is the work of Dale McGowan, one of the editors of this book. McGowan is the editor of *Parenting beyond Belief: On Raising Ethical, Caring Kids without Religion* and co-author of *Raising Freethinkers: A Practical Guide for Parenting beyond Belief.*[15] McGowan and his co-authors spell out the freedom that comes with raising children without indoctrination and advise parents on the most effective way to raise freethinking children. With advice from educators, doctors, psychologists, philosophers and parents, the book provides insights on a variety of topics from mixed marriages to coping with death and loss and from morality and ethics to dealing with holidays. *Raising*

13.   www.human.cornell.edu › HD › Outreach and Extension.
14.   www.skeptic.com/.
15.   Dale McGowan, *Parenting Beyond Belief: On Raising Ethical, Caring Kids without Religion* (New York: AMACOM, 2007); Dale McGowan, *et al.*, *Raising Freethinkers: A Practical Guide for Parenting Beyond Belief* (New York: AMACOM, 2009).

Freethinkers offers solutions to the challenges secular parents face and provides over 100 activities for both parents and children. The book covers every important topic secular parents need to know to help their children with their own moral and intellectual development, including advice on religious-extended-family issues, life and death, secular celebrations, wondering, questioning, and much more.

Furthermore, Arthur Dobrin's *Teaching Right from Wrong: 40 Things You Can Do to Raise a Moral Child.* Dobrin, a retired Ethical Culture leader and professor of humanities, offers a manual for raising ethical children and suggests using it not as a blueprint but as a guide. He also is the author of *Love your Neighbor: Stories of Values and Virtues*, a book that should be in every family's library.[16] In it he relates 13 original animal stories that teach about such values as friendship and cooperation, honesty and love, and respect for individuality. Dobrin ends each story with a provocative question parents can ask a child or a child can ponder alone.

Obligation to Bring Humanist Education to our Neighborhoods and our People

Returning to Joss Whedon's call, I interpret "our neighborhoods" and "our people" to mean our neighborhood schools, that is, public school and the people who attend them. One of our obligations is to support these schools in every way we can. However, it also should be noted that some parents are home-schooling their children because of religious intrusion into their public schools, the lack of strong science programs and critical thinking education, or bullying issues. That, of course, is their choice. Nonetheless, as defenders of strict church/state separation and secular government, we must defend secular public education by opposing voucher schemes to channel public funds to religious schools. Providing public funds to such schools undermines both secular government and secular education. However, there is more to say about what should happen *inside* public schools. In 2011 the American Humanist Association formulated "Ten Commitments: Guiding Principles for Teaching Values in America's Public Schools." This document begins by saying such values can and ought to be taught free of ideology and theology. To put it another way, "schools are responsible for developing literate and skilled human beings. But they also must be

16.   Arthur Dobrin, *Teaching Right from Wrong: 40 Things You Can Do to Raise a Moral Child* (New York: Berkley Trade, 2001) and Dobrin, *Love Your Neighbor: Stories of Values and Virtues* (New York: Scholastic, 2000).

committed to helping their students develop good personal, social, and citizenship values." The following are the ten principles that AHA believes serve as the moral foundation of education.

Altruism is the unselfish concern for the welfare of others without expectation of reward, recognition, or return. Opportunities for acts of altruism are everywhere in the family, the classroom, the school, and the wider community. Think of examples of altruistic acts in your experience. What person-to-person and group projects, classroom and school-wide activities, and community service projects might you and your students undertake?

Caring for the world around us. Everyone can and ought to play a role in caring for the Earth and its inhabitants. We can directly experience the living things in our homes and neighborhoods like trees, flowers, birds, insects, and pets. Gradually we expand our neighborhood. We learn about deserts and oceans, rivers and forests, the wild life around us and the wild life elsewhere. We learn that we are dependent on each other, on the natural world, and all that lives in it for food and shelter, space and beauty.

Critical thinking. We gain reliable knowledge because we are able to observe, report, experiment, and analyze what goes on around us. We also learn to raise questions that are clear and precise, to gather information, and to reason about the information we receive in a way that tests it for truthfulness, accuracy, and utility. From our earliest years we learn how to think and to share and challenge our ideas and the ideas of others, and consider their consequences. Practice asking "what next?" and "why?" and "how do I/you/we know that?"

Empathy. We human beings are capable of empathy, the ability to understand and enter imaginatively into another living being's feelings, the sad ones and the happy ones as well. Many of the personal relationships we have (in the family, among friends, between diverse individuals, and amid other living things) are made positive through empathy. With discussion and role-playing, we can learn how other people feel when they are sad or hurt or ignored, as well as when they experience great joys. We can use stories, anecdotes, and classroom events to help us nurture sensitivity to how our actions impact others.

Ethical development. Questions of fairness, cooperation, and sharing are among the first moral issues we encounter in our ethical development as human beings. Ethical education is ongoing implicitly and explicitly in what is called the "hidden curriculum" that we experience through the media, the family, and the community. Ethics can be taught through discussion, role-playing, storytelling, and other activities that improve analysis and decision-making regarding what's good and bad, right and wrong.

Global awareness. We live in a world that is rich in cultural, social, and individual diversity, a world where interdependence is increasing rapidly so that events anywhere are more likely to have consequences everywhere. Much can be done to prepare the next generation for accepting the responsibility of global citizenship. Understanding can be gained regarding the many communities in which we live through history, anthropology, and biology. A linguistic, ethnic, and cultural diversity are present in the classroom and provide lessons of diversity and commonality. We help others reach understanding about the interconnectedness of the welfare of all humanity.

Humility. We must always remember that there's a lot we don't know about the universe. There's still so very much to learn. Science will help us. But sometimes scientists discover surprising things that tell us how some of our old beliefs are false. So we need to be willing to change when our knowledge changes. A good humanist doesn't try to be sure of things that science can't show are true.

Peace and social justice. A curriculum that values and fosters peace education would promote the human rights of all people and understanding among all nations, cultural, and religious groups. Students should have opportunities to learn about the United Nations' role in preventing conflict as well as efforts to achieve social justice in the United States. They should learn about problems of injustice including what can be done to prevent and respond to these problems with meaningful actions that promote peace and social justice and that protect the inherent human rights of everyone both at home and abroad.

Responsibility. Our behavior is morally responsible when we tell the truth, help someone in trouble, and live up to promises we've made. Our behavior is legally responsible when we obey a just law and meet the requirements of membership or citizenship. But we also have a larger responsibility to be a caring member of our family, our community, and our world. Stories and role-playing can help students understand responsibility and its absence or failure. We learn from answering such questions as: What happens when we live in accordance with fair and just rules? What happens when we don't? What happens when the rules are unjust?

Service and participation. Life's fulfillment can emerge from an individual's participation in the service of humane ideals. School-based service learning combines community service objectives and learning objectives with the intent that the activities change both the recipient and the provider. It provides students with the ability to identify important issues in real-life situations. Through these efforts we learn that each of us can help meet the needs of others and of ourselves. Through our lifetime, we learn over and over again of our mutual dependence.

While these guiding principles were developed as principles for teaching values in our public schools, I believe they are the responsibility – obligation, if you will – of teachers everywhere and certainly of humanist parents.

Obligation to Bring Humanist Education to our World and Other Countries

I believe that it isn't just a question of *bringing* humanist education to the world and other countries. It is *joining* with fellow members of the International Humanist and Ethical Union (IHEU) in the more than 100 humanist, rationalist and freethought organizations in over 40 countries. The IHEU's stated mission, *our mission*, is to represent and support the worldwide humanist movement. The IHEU's stated aim, *our aim*, is to work toward building a world in which human rights are respected and everyone can live a life of dignity.

We can learn much from our overseas humanist brothers and sisters. Here is a brief example. When I was preparing the American Humanist Association's guidebook, *Establishing Humanist Education Programs for Children,* one of the first things I did was contact the British Humanist Association to ask what curriculum resources they have developed which they might share with us.[17] The resulting guidebook has a 26–page section that presents in great detail six of the toolkits the BHA developed for a range of age groups: "What Makes Us Special?" (for children ages 5–7); "What Do We

---

17.   http://www.americanhumanist.org/system/storage/63/d4/4/2129/childrens_
      manual_web.pdf.

Celebrate and Why?" and "How Should We Treat Other People and Why?" (both for children ages 7–11); "How Do You Know It's True?" "How Do You Tell Right From Wrong?" and "What's It All For?" (each for children ages 12–14). Thanks to the British Humanist Association, families on both sides of the Atlantic have a wealth of teaching resources on which to draw.

Furthermore, a section of the IHEU website, "The Humanist World," describes some of the programs humanists are involved in around the globe. For example, humanist organizations in Belgium and the Netherlands provide social and personal support through education, counseling and community care where hundreds of humanist educators and counselors are employed in schools, hospitals, prisons and the armed forces.[18] Humanist groups in Asia work for women's emancipation and the eradication of superstition, while humanists in Canada and Europe have fought for contraception and abortion rights. In Norway and the UK, humanist groups offer non-religious rites of passage (naming ceremonies, weddings and funerals) as a service to the humanist community. Still other international humanist groups fight for the separation of religion and government, and campaign against the genital mutilation of female children in Islamic societies.

In the end *education* itself is not enough. We must couple it with acting on our values and building humanist communities.

The Obligation to Act on our Values

In *Humanism as the Next Step*, Lloyd and Mary Morain cite humanist pioneer Oliver Reiser, author of *The Promise of Scientific Humanism*, who wrote, "our supreme responsibility is the moral obligation to be intelligent."[19] He believed that our obligation is to know what's going on in the world and to see, insofar as we can, that social change is headed in the right direction. To me this implies that we must *do* something to assure that social change *is* going in the right direction and not just talk about it. Corliss Lamont affirmed this in his 1949 book *The Philosophy of Humanism* when he wrote that "nothing is more important from an ethical viewpoint than teaching boys and girls, men and women, how to reason correctly *and to use their minds in dealing with the myriad problems of life*" (emphasis added).

18.   http://iheu.org/content/humanism-world-iheu-nutshell.
19.   Lloyd and Mary Morain, *Humanism as the Nest Step* (Washington, DC: Humanist Press, 2008), p. 90, citing Oliver L. Reiser, *The Promise of Scientific Humanism* (New York: Oskar Piest, 1940). Quotations are found at: http://americanhumanist.org/what_we_do/publications/Humanism_as_the_Next_Step /Chapter_7:_Applying_Humanism_to_Social_Problems.

To me, Lamont was saying that education is one dimension of humanism – acting on our values in dealing with the problems of life is another.[20]

How often have we heard – and have said ourselves – that humanism is focused on making this a better world. This is why humanists are concerned with issues of social justice, the eradication of poverty, and the peaceful resolution of conflicts. That is why, as a humanist, I believe we need to be activists as well as teachers. As a former coordinator of school-based service learning in Learn and Serve America, a program of the Corporation for National and Community Service, I see tremendous value in adults and children working together on community action projects.

Service learning is a strategy that integrates community service with instruction to enrich the learning experience, teach civic responsibility, and strengthen communities. I believe we should take a page out of the service-learning manuals and make community service a central part of humanist education. Such intergenerational partnerships were part of our program in the Corporation for National and Community Service. There is no reason why such partnerships cannot be part of humanist education program as well.

While I could recommend many resources, two of the most relevant are by Barbara A. Lewis: *The Kid's Guide to Service Projects* and *The Kid's Guide to Social Action*.[21] The subtitle of the former is "Over 500 Service Ideas for Young People Who Want to Make a Difference" and of the latter is "How to Solve the Social Problems You Choose – and Turn Creative Thinking into Positive Action." Both resources contain many examples of community action in a variety of area, for example, community development and beautification, the environment, homelessness and hunger, literacy, safety, and much more. There are many social problems to solve working side by side with the next generation.

Obligation to Build Humanist Communities

In the previously mentioned *Parenting beyond Belief*, community is described as the ability to surround oneself with an extended family, the members of which care for, support, nurture, and encourage each other's way through the

20.   Corliss Lamont, *The Philosophy of Humanism* (New York: Continuum, 1990), p. 248.

21.   Barbara A. Lewis, *The Kid's Guide to Service Projects: Over 500 Service Ideas for Young People Who Want to Make a Difference* (Minneapolis: Free Spirit Publishing, 1995) and *The Kid's Guide to Social Action: How to Solve the Social Problems You Choose – and Turn Creative Thinking into Positive Action* (Minneapolis: Free Spirit Publishing, 1998).

world and who lift each other up when any of them falls. The observation is made, however, that the effort to create secular community is in its infancy. Nevertheless, the objectives are clear and efforts are being made. Amanda Metskas, the director of Camp Quest and a contributor to *Raising Freethinkers: A Practical Guide for Parenting beyond Belief,* provides an important insight into building community when she writes: "It's about belonging. It's about acceptance. It's about mutual support and encouragement. Most of all, it speaks to needs beyond the intellectual into the emotional." She also offers a number of ways in which humanists can speak directly to this need and directs us to the following Parenting beyond Belief resources:

- *PBB* Facebook which now has over 5,600 members: www.facebook.com/pages/Parenting-Beyond-Belief/77773055518 (or go to Facebook and search "Parenting Beyond Belief").
- A Facebook group for secular mothers (Mothers Beyond Belief, www.facebook.com/groups/mothersbeyondbelief) and secular fathers (Dads Beyond Belief, www.facebook.com/groups/dadsbeyondbelief)
- A list of local secular parenting groups: http://parentingbeyondbelief.com/parents/
- A list of secular parenting blogs: http://parentingbeyondbelief.com/blog/

Since it's never too early to build community, Amanda also discusses ways to create a children's program and suggests that it's best to start with small, simple steps.

I, too, have suggested steps in establishing such programs in the Kochhar Humanist Education Center's 2011 publication, *Establishing Humanist Education Programs for Children.*[22] The steps are assessing needs, determining objectives, advertising the program, establishing policies, acquiring funds, determining the curriculum, identifying resources, implementing the program, and evaluating it.

On a related note, one of the most eloquent statements on building community can be found in Bart Ehrman's speech in acceptance of the AHA's 2011 Religious Liberty award (adapted into an article titled, "Biblical Scholarship and the Right to Know," in the November/December 2011 issue of the *Humanist*). In part, Ehrman said: "When someone leaves the womb of the church, they need to have somewhere else to go. They need

22.   http://www.americanhumanist.org/system/storage/63/d4/4/2129/childrens_manual_web.pdf.

warm, loving, welcoming, safe communities of like-minded people where they can establish social networks and find fellowship with people who share their worldviews… They need places where they can celebrate what is good in life and where they can work to overcome what is bad." Ehrman contends, "Humanist organizations need to become as recognizable as the Baptist church on the corner and the Episcopal church up the street."[23] In short, I would say that we must work toward building both a physical community and a psychological community for us – and for the next generation.

Since no single humanist group can address this obligation by itself, we must collaborate. Fortunately we do not have to reinvent the wheel. A coalition already exists, the Secular Coalition for America.[24] *Its* members are American Atheists, American Ethical Union, American Humanist Association, Atheist Alliance of America, Camp Quest, Council for Secular Humanism, Institute for Humanist Studies, Military Association of Atheists and Freethinkers, Secular Student Alliance, and the Society for Humanistic Judaism. Additionally, over 30 organizations have extended their support by endorsing the mission of the SCA. I suggest that the organizations in the coalition join together in further developing educational programs for children and youth. Several ethical culture societies of the American Ethical Union already have such programs that have marvelous teaching resources and years of experience. We can learn much from them. Camp Quest "provides children of freethinking parents a residential summer camp dedicated to improving the human condition through rational inquiry, critical and creative thinking, scientific method, self-respect, ethics, competency, democracy, free speech, and the separation of religion and government."[25]

Their many goals are totally consistent with the obligations to the next generation; in fact, they are the same: to build a community for freethinking families; foster curiosity, questioning, and critical thinking; encourage reason and compassion as foundations of an ethical, productive and fulfilling life; raise awareness of positive contributions made by atheists, agnostics, humanists, freethinkers, and other nontheists to society; promote an open dialogue about philosophical questions that is marked by challenging each other's ideas while at the same time treating each other with respect; and demonstrate atheism and humanism as positive, family-friendly worldviews. Those are the goals of Camp Quest; they should be the goals of all humanist groups.

23.   The entire text of Bart Ehrman's talk is at:http://thehumanist.org/november-december-2011/biblical-scholarship-and-the-right-to-know/ (p. 20).

24.   SCA, www.secular.org/.

25.   *campquest.org/.*

While we may not have a legal obligation to educate humanistically, we surely have a moral one. I suggest that we *pledge* to educate our children using all the resources we have on hand; act on our humanist values together *with* our children; and work with our fellow humanists to build humanist communities *with and for* our children. I believe "everyday humanists" have these three obligations to the next generation: education, education, education (as Joss Whedon asserted) along with action and community building. By pursuing these, I believe we can best nurture humanist values in the hearts and minds of the next generation.

6 Humanism and the Expression of Love

Anne Klaeysen[*]

"I know of only one duty, and that is to love."

Albert Camus

Contrary to popular perceptions, humanism maintains a deep regard for the emotionally charged connections between individuals and groups. It has an abiding interest in and response to the nature of human life meaning revolving around practices of love. This chapter provides attention to the manner in which humanism informs and influences the nature and meaning of human connection.

Personal Reflection – a Starting Point

Humanism is, for me, the ultimate expression of love. There is no need for a supernatural intermediary in human relationships. I do not see "god" in the other; indeed, that would obscure, not reveal, love. My religion of Ethical

---

[*] Anne Klaeysen, in addition to her work at New York Society of Ethical Culture, was the first Humanist Chaplain at Adelphi University in Garden City, NY and now serves the Barnard College community at Columbia University as Humanist Religious Life Advisor. A graduate of the Humanist Institute, she is now co-Dean of the Institute. Klaeysen was Leader of the Ethical Humanist Society of Long Island from 2002 to 2008. She holds a Doctor of Ministry degree from Hebrew Union College, Master's degrees in Business Administration from New York University and in German from the State University of New York at Albany, and studied at the University of Wuerzburg in Germany. Klaeysen represents the American Ethical Union on the Board of Governors of the Religious Coalition for Reproductive Choice and is an active participant in Empire State Pride in the Pulpit, New Yorkers Against the Death Penalty, the Interfaith Peace Alliance, and Women's International League for Peace and Freedom.

Humanism offers the most direct and meaningful connection between individuals and among groups, opening up possibilities for creating loving communities.[1]

Many people find humanism as adults, having grown up in a different (or no) faith tradition and spending years exploring the contemporary religious landscape. It's easier in the twenty-first century to find because so much information is readily available online. They are drawn to the philosophy, decide that they have really been humanists all their lives, and look for others who think the same way.

When they come through the doors of an Ethical Society, they also discover how humanism *feels*, how we practice a nontheistic religion of ethics on a daily basis. It starts with a thought and a desire to meet "like-minded people." It can turn into a homecoming: joining a community devoted to learning how to live a meaningful life filled with love and concern for others.

Since each of us travels different winding roads, I begin with my journey to humanism, to a vocation that led me to serve as Leader to the New York Society for Ethical Culture (NYSEC). Our congregation on the Upper West Side of Manhattan has 200 members and twice as many friends, a category sometimes referred to as "fellow travelers" who are commitment-shy but come to us for life passage ceremonies and workshops. Humanists are fiercely independent and "traditional" non-joiners. It's a wonder that we have as many humanist groups as we do!

I grew up in a village in western New York on the banks of the Erie Canal. The Irish who dug the canal and the Dutch who planted orchards between the canal and Lake Ontario reared generations of Americans, two of whom married and became my parents. It was a mixed marriage – Catholic and

---

1.   "Religion is a set of beliefs and/or institutions, behaviors and emotions which binds human beings to something beyond their individual selves and fosters in its adherents a sense of humility and gratitude that, in turn, sets the tone of one's worldview and requires certain behavioral dispositions relative to that which transcends personal interested. In other words, religion connects a person with a larger world and creates a loyalty that extends to the past, the present and the future. This loyalty not only makes demands upon the person but – and this is the part that makes it distinctly spiritual – it creates a sense of humility. So religion provides a story about one's place in the larger scheme of things, creates a sense of connection and it makes one feel grateful" (Arthur Dobrin, Ethical Humanist Leader, 2000). See Dobrin, "Religious Ethics: A Source Book," p. 6; http://arthurdobrin.files.wordpress.com/2008/08/religious-ethics.pdf. Ethical Culture and Ethical Humanism are synonymous. Some societies and fellowships within the American Ethical Union (AEU) also refer to themselves as simply "Ethical."

Protestant, and we four children were raised Catholic, to the bitter disappointment of my Dutch Reformed grandparents.

Memories can be long: my Irish grandmother never forgave the English for the potato famine in the mid-nineteenth century, and my Dutch grandmother held a grudge against Catholics who conquered the Netherlands in the sixteenth century. They lived next door to one another on West Foster Street, and that's where my parents met.

With fewer than four thousand inhabitants, Palmyra supported a dozen churches and as many bars. This is perhaps explained by history: in the early 1800s, the village and its environs were part of what was called the "Burned-Over District," where so many religious revivals were held that by the end of the century there was no more "fuel" (the unconverted) to "burn" (convert). Joseph Smith, founder of Mormonism in 1830, grew up on the same country road as I did. The three Fox sisters "rapped" to communicate with "the other side" and founded Spiritualism that continued long after one of them recanted. The first Women's Rights Convention was held in 1848 a few miles east in Seneca Falls. Alongside Elizabeth Cady Stanton stood Frederick Douglass, then publisher of the abolitionist paper *The North Star* in Rochester, calling for women's suffrage as loudly as he called for freedom from slavery. A few miles to the south in Dundee, Robert Ingersoll was becoming the Great Agnostic. And I imagine the Great Peacemaker, who united the warring Iroquois tribes into a confederacy centuries earlier, still walking among the lakes and forests of his people.

I brought this family and regional history with me to the State University of New York at Albany where, as a freshman, I met another tribe: New York City Jews. One of them became my best friend, and years later, after we had moved to Brooklyn, I married him at the Brooklyn Society for Ethical Culture. Our mixed marriage, officiated by an Ethical Culture Leader in the library, was very different from my parents' formal affair at the altar of St Anne's Church where a priest presided. No religious conversion was required, just a sincere expression of love and commitment.

Glenn and I didn't formally join the Brooklyn Society until we had children. Living far from their grandparents, we wanted them to experience an extended family. A quotation from Felix Adler, who founded Ethical Culture in 1876, confirmed our choice: "We should teach our children nothing which they shall ever need to unlearn; we should strive to transmit to them the best possessions, the truest thought, the noblest sentiments of the age in which we live."[2] *That's* what I wanted for Andrew and Emily. And,

---

2.   Felix Adler, *Life and Destiny*, "Ethical Outlook – Section 9" (New York: McClure, Phillips, and Co., 1913).

for myself, I found a new way of thinking about ethics that involved real commitment:

- I choose to attribute worth and dignity to every human being.
- I choose to treat people as ends unto themselves, with their own aspirations, and not as a means to further my own goals.
- I strive to act in ways that elicit the best, the unique excellence and indispensable quality, in others, and thereby in myself.

This practice, unlike the proverbial "Golden Rule" – "do unto others as you would have them do unto you" – is active, not passive; it demands ethical engagement and is the loving work of a lifetime.

Over the years I became an active member, and 15 years ago embarked on training for Ethical Humanist leadership with the American Ethical Union. After completing my studies, I interned at the New York Society and later served the Ethical Humanist Society of Long Island in Garden City, New York for six years. While there, I also became the first Humanist Chaplain at Adelphi University. As of the writing of this chapter, I'm chaplain at both Columbia and New York Universities. For me, there is no better way to express my love for others and to work with them to build loving communities than to serve as a leader.

Having provided my personal narrative as context for a larger discussion of love, in the following sections of this chapter, I will discuss ways in which humanism sheds light upon the nature of love, finds meaning in its existence, and celebrates human connections.

Humanist Concept of Love

No one can live out of the light and warmth of love; it is the very essence of our humanity and, therefore, is the core of humanism. Rather than worship a deity presumed to be the source of perfect love, we embrace one another with all our imperfections and make connections in pursuit of better understanding this life and giving our lives meaning. It is in ethical engagement that we realize our potential for love – and creativity.

The first Humanist Manifesto (1933) states, "Believing that religion must work increasingly for joy in living, religious humanists aim to foster the creative in man and to encourage achievements that add to the satisfactions of life."[3] Love is not something that "happens" to us; it is an achievement of

3.   "Humanist Manifesto I," American Humanist Association, accessed December 2, 2013, http://americanhumanist.org/Humanism/Humanist_Manifesto_I.

the human heart that dares to reach out to another human being, or group of people, to create relationships both vulnerable and strong. Even when we have not experienced unconditional love in our families of origin, we still have the potential to receive and give love to others. Indeed, that is our obligation as human beings. The men who forged this "new philosophy" asserted that hhumanism would "(a) affirm life rather than deny it; (b) seek to elicit the possibilities of life, not flee from them; and (c) endeavor to establish the conditions of a satisfactory life for all, not merely for the few."[4] It was their hope that this perspective would guide future efforts and inspire new practices.

Forty years later, a second Humanist Manifesto, signed by both women and men, held that "The preciousness and dignity of the individual person is a central humanist value. Individuals should be encouraged to realize their own creative talents and desires."[5] Furthermore, "Happiness and the creative realization of human needs and desires, individually and in shared enjoyment, are continuous themes of humanism."[6] What a resounding affirmation of love! We meet one another as whole selves, respecting our differences and connecting in healthy relationships that enhance our lives. No supernatural or otherworldly source need be called upon to create love. It is ours by virtue of our humanity.

The latest, but surely not the last, Humanist Manifesto, introduced in 2003, again "affirms our ability and responsibility to lead ethical lives of personal fulfillment that aspire to the greater good of humanity."[7] Humanism is a life-stance "guided by reason, inspired by compassion, and informed by experience" that "encourages us to live life well and fully." This document explicitly refers to our striving "toward a world of mutual care and concern, free of cruelty and its consequences, where differences are resolved cooperatively without resorting to violence." It is interdependence that "encourages us to enrich the lives of others, and inspires hope of attaining peace, justice, and opportunity for all."[8] There is no better definition of love and its workings. We humans are called upon by our very nature to create loving community. It is only through this experience of ethical engagement that we become fully human and completely ourselves. "I am because we are" is a saying attributed to the Ubuntu concept in African spirituality that we are all connected and cannot truly be ourselves without community. One's

4.   "Humanist Manifesto I."
5.   "Humanist Manifesto II," American Humanist Association, accessed December 2, 2013, http://americanhumanist.org/Humanism/Humanist_Manifesto_II.
6.   "Humanist Manifesto II."
7.   "Humanist Manifesto III," American Humanist Association, accessed December 2, 2013, http://americanhumanist.org/Humanism/Humanist_Manifesto_III.
8.   "Humanist Manifesto III."

wellbeing is inextricably linked with the wellbeing of others. Love is indeed the path that humanism offers.

In my work as pastoral counselor, I am inspired by what two humanist psychoanalysts – Erich Fromm and Matthew Ies Spetter – have written about love. In his most popular book, *The Art of Loving*, Fromm recasts love as "an activity, not a passive affect"[9] whose basic elements are "care, responsibility, respect and knowledge."[10] Healthy adults use reason, as well as emotions, to develop a humility that allows them to outgrow a child's dreams of omniscience and omnipotence. We learn to listen even as we yearn to be heard, and strive to live fully in the present with others. We also develop a faith in our ability to love and be loved, a faith in the potential in ourselves and in others. "Society," asserts Fromm, "must be organized in such a way that man's social, loving nature is not separated from his social existence, but becomes one with it." Indeed, "love is the only sane and satisfactory answer to the problem of human existence."[11]

Fromm's ancestry included rabbis, and as a young man, he studied the Talmud with his uncle and other scholars while also studying law at Frankfurt University and then sociology, philosophy and psychology at the University of Heidelberg. He later applied secular interpretations to scripture, developing a humanistic philosophy to explain the biblical myth of the exile from the Garden of Eden. In *Escape from Freedom*, it is the story of human evolution: Adam and Eve, aware of themselves as both separate from and part of nature, establish their own moral values and develop their own powers of reason and love. So, too, are we both separate from and part of society. Departing from Freud, he concluded that "man is primarily a social being" and that "the key problem of psychology is that of the particular kind of relatedness of the individual toward the world, not that of satisfaction or frustration of single instinctual desires."[12]

The coming of the Nazis to power in 1933 forced Fromm to move first to Switzerland and then to the United States. Throughout World War II, he tried to enlighten the American public about the real intentions and perils of Nazism. Spetter experienced Nazism firsthand. Born in the Netherlands, he participated in the Dutch and French resistance during the war and was arrested in 1943. He was condemned to death because of his work on behalf of Allied Intelligence and was a prisoner at the Buchenwald and Auschwitz

9.   Erich Fromm, *The Art of Loving* (New York: Harper & Row, 1956), p. 22.
10.   Fromm, *Art of Loving*, p. 26.
11.   Fromm, *Art of Loving*, p. 133.
12.   Erich Fromm, *Escape from Freedom* (New York: Holt, Rinehart & Winston, 1941), p. 290.

concentration camps. After his liberation, Spetter served in the Dutch Security Branch of the US Army and was a witness at the International War Criminal Trials on Nuremburg, Germany. He was awarded the Resistance Cross by the Government of the Netherlands. In his book, *Man the Reluctant Brother*, Spetter writes, "I have only one theme: it is to expose the mutilation of the human person. I have only one cause: to arouse my generation against those paralyzing trends which make pawns out of people, and so to help rescue the human heart in which I believe."[13] For him, the humanist idea of love was "to accept the fact that all life is marred by imperfection and that nevertheless, we must be loyal and struggle with our differences, and injuries while keeping a thirst for decency alive."[14] Love reaches for communion with others, sustaining the belief that although each of us is a unique personality, still we are not alone.

When I listen to a member of my congregation or a student who comes to me for pastoral counseling, I often recall my mentor's wisdom in these words: "The problems of life do not wear us out; it is the shortage of love that does... We are happiest when we share, work together, eat together (passing food around, not hoarding it)."[15] And I hear his gentle Dutch voice reminding me that "The essence of love is that, while it may be obscured and almost deadened, it can also be stirred from its arrest, by the simplicity of a word or a glimpse of hope."[16] His humanist credo was that human beings have the capacity to respond to truth and one's own conscience and that love involves a mutuality of respect, allowing us to "become more ourselves than we ever were before."[17] He stressed, above all, a life of compassion.

I close this section with a poem by Ellen Bass, who poignantly expresses a faith in, and commitment to, life:

> "The Thing Is"[18]
> to love life, to love it even
> when you have no stomach for it
> and everything you've held dear
> crumbles like burnt paper in your hands,

13.   Matthew Ies Spetter, *Man the Reluctant Brother* (New York: The Fieldston Press, 1967), p. 7.
14.   Spetter, *Man the Reluctant Brother*, p. 37.
15.   Spetter, *Man the Reluctant Brother*, p. 117.
16.   Spetter, *Man the Reluctant Brother*, p. 221.
17.   Spetter, *Man the Reluctant Brother*, p. 228.
18.   Bass, Ellen, *Mules of Love* (Rochester, New York: BOA Editions, 2002). Ellen Bass, "The Thing Is" from Mules of Love, copyright © 2002 by Ellen Bass, reprinted with the permission of The Permissions Company, on behalf of BOA Editions Ltd, www.boaeditions.org.

your throat filled with the silt of it.
When grief sits with you, its tropical heat
thickening the air, heavy as water
more fit for gills than lungs;
when grief weights you like your own flesh
only more of it, an obesity of grief,
you think, *How can a body withstand this?*
Then you hold life like a face
between your palms, a plain face,
no charming smile, no violet eyes,
and you say, yes, I will take you
I will love you, again.

Celebrating Love[19]

What makes a humanist ceremony different from traditional religious ceremonies? In this section, I'll answer that question with examples from weddings, baby namings and memorial services. Essentially it involves a process of listening to the couples and families talk about their relationships and reflecting back what I hear them say about love. Together we create a meaningful public event that expresses that love.

Weddings

Couples find me in several ways: referrals from family and friends, online searches, even at the City Clerk's office where NYSEC is mentioned in the state domestic relations law. Many come from different family, faith and cultural traditions; most call themselves "spiritual but not religious"[20] or SBNR, an acronym coined by the Pew Research Religion & Public Life Project.

Below are parts of a ceremony I have honed over the years. I emphasize not only the love between the couple, but also their relationships with families and friends. My collection of wedding readings has expanded as couples contribute new ones. A reading that surprised me was from *The Velveteen Rabbit.*[21] I couldn't imagine it working, but it did, especially when the

---

19.   National Leaders Council, "Life Passage Ceremonies" (New York: American Ethical Union, 2002).

20.   "'Nones' on the Rise: Religion and the Unaffiliated," October 9, 2012, http://www.pewforum.org/2012/10/09/nones-on-the-rise-religion/.

21.   Margery Williams, *The Velveteen Rabbit (or How Toys Become Real)*, (New York: George H. Doran Co., 1922).

children of one couple (his daughter, her son) read it together as a dialogue between the rabbit and his friend, the horse. There wasn't a dry eye in the house.

Before we meet, I email the draft and suggest that the couple play with it and read the words, especially the vows, aloud to one another. At the first meeting, I tell them, "I assume that you're married already. You've made the most important commitment to one another personally and privately. Now it's time to develop a public statement. I'm the non-anxious presence facilitating your creative process. Remember: You can't do anything wrong. Everyone loves you, even if they don't always know how to show it, and they're happy to be celebrating with you."

Then I ask questions: How did you first meet? What do you most admire about your partner? What is involved in your decision to marry? Tell me the story of your love. I listen deeply, almost like a meditation, breathing in their words and feelings. Humor is important. A couple that doesn't laugh together, doesn't get each other's jokes and doesn't have inside jokes is a couple in trouble. They ask me questions, too, usually about humanism and Ethical Culture, and often return after the wedding to learn more.

At the end of our first visit, my parting words are, "Now go home and think about your ceremony. Everything we say must reflect who you are and what your relationship really is. Not everything will be perfect, but it must feel right." Over the next weeks, we engage in a process that involves more meetings, emails and phone calls, creating together a meaningful expression of their shared love.

One groom recently asked me a question that I had never before been asked: "How's *your* marriage?" I burst out laughing. What a great question! I wondered why no one had asked me that before. I began my answer with a story about a colleague who realized that every time she met with a couple or officiated at a wedding, she hated to go home. She was miserable in her marriage, and witnessing so much happiness made her confront that reality. How could it not? We are not mere celebrants who recite magical incantations; ours is a weighty responsibility to shepherd a couple through a process that focuses on their relationship. In that process, we examine our own. I enjoy going home and telling Glenn about the latest couple I have met: two people who, like us, found each other, worked to build a loving relationship, and are now taking a courageous leap into the future together.

WELCOME

Welcome. My name is Anne Klaeysen, and I am Leader of the New York Society for Ethical Culture. As you know, Dearly Beloved, we are gathered here today to celebrate the wedding ceremony of _____ and _____ .

As couples have done for some thousands of years, these two come before you, their wedding community, to make their pledges to each other. They come before you to make an ancient promise that binds the wedding couple across all previous boundaries. They come before you to join their two lives in marriage.

In the Ethical Culture wedding ceremony we encourage the couple to find and share words that come, for them, as close as possible to the joint truths of this event. This _____ and _____ have done.

READINGS
Poems, songs, essays, family sayings and writings, personal statements, etc. selected to give special meaning to the ceremony and/ or to provide a family member or friend with a role.

OFFICIANT'S WORDS
I am very pleased to be here today and would like to share some wedding thoughts with you. Why marry? Why not just live together and love each other without a public declaration? What makes today remarkable?

First of all, _____ and _____ love each other. That much is obvious. No ceremony can create a human relationship; it can only recognize, and celebrate, an existing relationship. These are people who share the same values, who delight in each other's company more than any other's, who together are somehow more than they are apart, and who promise, at life's most critical juncture, to help each other deepen and heighten their own best selves. You and I are also involved in that promise. We have the right and the responsibility to hold them to their vows, to help them struggle against the voices of modern distraction. What is it to marry because you love? What is it to stay loving because you have married? These things are mysteries. The work of questions such as these is also an obligation assumed by the heart and the will according to the promises made today.

Across many centuries, traditions, geography and generations, weddings take place at the heart of the world. In the smallest hamlet and the largest metropolis, people are getting married, and people who love them are in attendance. The best hope of the world is represented in this community of beloved families and friends here gathered, perhaps at some sacrifice, to wish this couple well. Look around. Though we may not all know one another, still we are members now of the same wedding community, family in an extended sense, sharing our love for this couple and our hopes for the success of their life partnership.

Secondly, a wedding ceremony is a unique opportunity for a couple to openly declare their personal feelings and to share with us, the wedding community, what is most important to them. What *is* most important to _____ and _____?

(Shared thoughts from interview and meetings with the couple: what is most important and meaningful, how they experience and appreciate each other, etc.)

VOWS AND EXCHANGE OF RINGS

Vows may be read or repeated after the celebrant. This consti-tutes the legal contract and must be witnessed by those chosen to sign the marriage license. Here are two samples. (Couples may, of course, write their own vows.

I, _____, take you, _____, to be my wedded wife/husband/partner, to have and to hold, for richer and for poorer, in sickness and in health, for the rest of our days.

I, _____, take you, _____, to be my wife/hus-band/partner. I give you my hand and my heart. I pledge to share my life openly with you and to speak loving truth to you. I promise to respect and honor you, care for you in tenderness, support you with patience and love, and walk with you through all the seasons of our lives.

"Rings are an ancient symbol,
blessed and simple. Round like the sun,
like the eye, like arms that embrace.
Circles, for love that is given
comes back round again and again.
Therefore, may these symbols
remind you that your love, like the sun,
illumines; that your love,
like the eye, must see clearly;
and that your love,
like arms that embrace,
is a grace upon this world."
With this ring, I thee wed, and bind my life to yours.

DECLARATION

By the power of your choice and the words that you have spoken to each other, I do declare that from this moment forward you are married, and you may now kiss one another.

We wish for _____ and _____ such goodwill and respect towards one another, and such support from others, that they may grow stronger in their love and be able to turn every crisis and challenge into an opportunity for the renewal and deepening of their relationship.

In Ethical Culture, we say, "The place where we meet to seek the highest is holy ground." Today in this place, at this time, we have truly sought the highest and together shared holy ground.

****

Baby welcoming/naming

Our children were welcomed to the community and publicly given their names before family and friends in ceremonies at the Brooklyn Society for Ethical Culture. Their grandparents, who hoped for baptisms or, in the case of our son, a *bris*, were good sports and recited the readings we gave them. The beauty of humanist ceremonies is the opportunity to do it yourself. There are no rules, only a sincere expression of love and commitment. Here is what I wrote for our son:

> Two years ago most of you here celebrated our wedding with us. Since then our family has grown. We have a son – Andrew.
>
> The day I married Glenn was the happiest day of my life. Another was the day Andrew was born. All three of us worked as a team: Andrew was awake and kicking; I reeled from some of the contractions; and Glenn, our steadfast coach, encouraged us both.I've told some of you that when the doctor placed Andrew on my abdomen I asked her not to cut the umbilical cord. It's true that I was afraid to let him go, but what I want for Andrew is to be himself, to know who he is, and to be strong and independent.
>
> Glenn and I have discussed the values we want to give Andrew. Among them are reason and compassion. We want him to be able to think clearly and to come to his own reasoned decisions. We also want him to understand and feel empathy for his fellow human beings.
>
> We ask you, his family and community, to support us and to help Andrew become Andrew.

Glenn wrote a limerick:

> A couple whose love ran so deep,
> Each gave the other to keep.

They had their fun,
Then had a son.
Now they can't get any sleep.

At our daughter's ceremony, I spoke directly to her:

> Being a second child isn't easy, perhaps because comparison with the older sibling comes so easily. So I promise you, Emily, that I will remember that you are your own unique independent self. Actually, this won't be a hard promise to keep. You started asserting yourself *in utero*, and I don't expect you to stop. I hope you don't.
>
> You are only three weeks old, but I feel I have known you forever. You are strong, strong-willed and vibrant. You teach us more about yourself every day.
>
> As I have welcomed you into my heart, I now welcome you into this circle of family and friends. We will love you, nurture you and support you.

When I officiate for families, I ask them to think about whether they want a private ceremony at home or a public one with their community. What values do they wish to communicate? What gifts, tangible and intangible, do they wish to give their child? What roles will their family and friends play? A humanist baby naming ceremony may include parent and or/ community vows. Here is an example.

> To be a parent forces you to recognize that you are no longer a child. No matter how childish and childlike you feel, to your child you still remain the parent, his or her authority on life. When you look at your children, you may see yourself in them and feel the temptation to help them succeed where you have failed. But as much as we seek to make them like us, they are unique. What we can do is encourage them to do their best. As they grow, they will push us to grow, too, and to do our best. This we can do, if we love them not for whom they may become, but who they are, and accept who we are – both our strengths and weaknesses.
>
> "Parenthood is also a serious expression and severe test of a marriage. The greatest act of love parents have to give their children is the love they express for one another. Interactions between mother and father, wife and husband, form the web of relationships that serve as a family nest.
>
> Recognizing this, _____ and _____ , you stand before us now to reaffirm your commitment to each other and your

daughter/son. Do you, _____ , commit yourself to _____
as her husband/his wife (or her/his partner) to support her/him
as a mother/father? Dou you give yourself to your child as her/
his mother/father, promising to act out of love, respecting her/his
uniqueness and eliciting the best from her/him?

I often quote Ethical Culture founder Felix Adler: "The love of the parent
is the warm nest for the fledgling spirit of the child. To be at home in this
strange world, the young being… must find somewhere a place where he is
welcomed without regard to usefulness or merit. It is the love of the parents
that makes the home, and it is his own home that makes the child at home
in the world."[22] We teach our children to see themselves both as individuals
and invaluable members of our community. Every day they learn, together
with us, how to be more human: how to experience empathy and express
compassion. Of course, like all humanist ceremonies, baby namings are
also filled with music, poetry and laughter.

Memorials

Since becoming an Ethical Humanist Leader, too many dear members of
my congregations have died. It was a privilege to be with them through the
process of their dying and to honor them in memorial services. I hope that I
will be able to face my own death with such strength and grace. Some members meet with me to talk about the services they would like and what roles
their family and friends should play. It gives them an opportunity to reflect
upon their lives and is also a gift to their survivors. I recall the children of
one woman who were inconsolable at her death because they didn't know
what to do. Fortunately, she had left clear instructions, including music and
readings, and I was able to guide them through the memorial process.

As I sat at the bedside of another woman in hospice, a nurse came in and
told her not to be afraid. Without skipping a beat, Moira replied, "Afraid?
Why would I be afraid? I'm dying, that's all." She also kicked a chaplain
out of her room who apparently thought Moira should be more distraught
than she was, given that she didn't believe in either a god or an afterlife.
Humanists harbor no illusions about death. We cherish life and live it to the
fullest, carrying in our hearts memories of those who have died.

When my mother-in-law died, we held her memorial at the Brooklyn
Society. As I described the process of planning it, a neighbor said, somewhat

---

22.   Felix Adler, *An Ethical Philosophy of Life* (New York: D. Appleton-Century
Co., 1918), p. 252.

archly, "It sounds like you're planning a wedding, not a funeral." Indeed, it was a celebration of Muriel's life, and her family rejoiced that she had lived and loved as long as she had. One of her sons played her favorite song, "Always," written by Irving Berlin for his wife, on the piano. Her grandchildren read tributes they had written to her. I read a letter that her husband Stanley, who predeceased her, wrote to her mother extolling his beloved's virtues. Once again, there wasn't a dry eye in the house. There were tears of both sorrow and joy.

I also officiate at services for people who never joined our community, but whose families feel that they shared our values, making a humanist service more appropriate than a traditionally religious one. Again I send them a draft (excerpts below), as well as readings, and offer myself as the non-anxious presence facilitating their creative process. It is a humbling and deeply moving experience to listen to their stories.

Opening Words and Welcome
Good morning/afternoon. My name is Anne Klaeysen, and I am Leader of the New York Society for Ethical Culture. I welcome you into this time and space that are made sacred with the spirit of love and friendship you bring as you gather to remember and mourn _____. We come together as family, friends, neighbors, and colleagues: co-creators of a community that includes those present but also family and friends who could not be here today.

A memorial service is an act of loving leave-taking and a celebration of life. We don't need protection from grief, but rather time and the means to express it, to experience it, and to live through it. A memorial service is for those who have loved and lost, who miss loved ones and must go on living without them. Shakespeare wrote in Macbeth: "Give sorrow words. The grief that does not speak/Whispers the o'erfraught heart and bids it break."

This morning/afternoon we will give sorrow words: some of you will share your memories; others will sit quietly and reflect; together we will invoke _____'s spirit and celebrate his/her life.

Memorial Portrait and Readings
This part combines shared memories and readings by selected family and friends.

Shared Memories Circle
During the next few minutes, I invite you to share something of what it has meant to you to experience _____'s compan-

ionship, wisdom or humor in your own lives. You may wish to share a memory or say something about how your life has been enriched by her/him. In this way, we make _____ present among us. If there are silent spaces between speakers, we can use this time to nourish a silent memory.

Closing
Felix Adler, founder of Ethical Culture said "The dead are not dead if we have loved them truly. In our own lives we can give them a kind of immortality. Let us arise and take up the work they have left unfinished." Take a moment to remember what you most admired about _____. Remember what most endeared him/ her to you. Have it? Good. Hold on to it. Now imagine incorporating that quality, that gift into your own life. Love him/her, honor him/her, give him/her immortality by taking up the work he/she has left unfinished.

> The act is done. The words have been said.
> The gate of the coming hour
> now opens to us in peace.
> Let us go through with thanksgiving for all that we said and did in this hour.
> Blessed is the mystery of life and death, which is our own.
> And blessed be Love forever.

Conclusion

Love is the essence of Humanism, and it's expressed in myriad ways through our philosophy and practices. Every day offers us opportunities to reflect upon the nature of our relationships and our goals. With deeply felt and reasonable intention we choose to give our lives meaning through love – daring to be vulnerable and learning to be strong in loving communion with others.

7 Personal Reflection on Humanist Memorial Services

Susan Rose[*]

Context: Personal Experience

5:25 am – December 19, 1989 – the phone rings. It is the hospital. My mother has died after three weeks of being in a coma. Among other things, I feel relief because the doctors have informed me that there is no chance that she will ever recover any brain function. Although my mother told me that she doesn't want any "heroic" measures taken to keep her alive in such a situation, I have nothing in writing and the hospital would not allow the artificial respiration and the artificial nutrition she was receiving to be discontinued. The best I could do for my mother was to fight to get a "Do Not Resuscitate" order signed. That took well over a week, and a visit to the hospital from a lawyer friend. Things were different back then.

5:35 am – December 19, 1989 – I call the Clergy Leader of the Ethical Culture Society to which I belong. Although I was raised in Ethical Culture from the age of three, and at this point have been a member as an adult for many years, I have never before this moment been so sure of why it is good to belong to a congregation; I can call the Leader to tell him that my mother died.

10 am or so – December 19, 1989 – another reason to belong to a congregation. The Leader of my Society meets me at the morgue of the hospital

---

[*] Susan Rose was active in the Ethical Culture Society of Essex County, serving as President from 1988–1990. She served on the National Board of the American Ethical Union for five years and the National Membership Committee for over ten years. Susan was certified as an Ethical Culture Leader in 1999 and has served the Ethical Movement in various capacities, including Dean of the Leadership Training Program. Susan is also the Dean of the American Ethical Union Leadership Training Program and serves on the Assembly Planning Committee of the American Ethical Union. She serves on the Humanist Institute Board.

(Coney Island Hospital, Brooklyn, New York) for a final viewing of my mom. He goes in first and makes sure that there isn't a sheet covering my mom's face when I go in to see her. I have no trouble seeing her dead, in fact she looks far more peaceful than she had for the previous three weeks with air being pumped into her and a tube inserted in her nose, but I don't want to see her with a sheet over her face. She's in a drawer at the morgue. That's enough with which to deal.

7 pm or so – still December 19, 1989 – my living room in Elizabeth, New Jersey. The Leader of my Society has come to visit me at home, and to begin some preliminary planning for the memorial service. That's what he tells me. Years later I understand that this visit serves a practical purpose and in addition, through the process of gathering information about my mother's life – a life review – he has facilitated my grieving process. I get to reflect on my mother's life, to think of all of the activism in her life and what was important to her.

A day or so later – there is a visit from a member of the Ethical Society to which I belong. He brings coffee and toilet paper. What more might one need – a humanist version of the Jewish custom of sitting Shiva?

December 22, 1989 – there is a memorial for my mom, Anita Frater, at the Ethical Culture Society of Essex County. She would have liked it, especially the flowers. I remember they were vivid, striking, and there was one glorious bird-of-paradise. There were no carnations, a flower my mother didn't like much. Friends and family, and members of my congregation gathered to share their memories of my mom, or, for those who had never met her, their support for me.

I don't remember a whole lot about the memorial service for my mother. I remember the flowers and that there was coffee and pastries I guess – similar to a Sunday morning coffee hour and that seemed appropriate. However, what I remember most was a sense of not being alone, that there were people who cared about me and would help me, who gave me very useful advice, and some perhaps not so useful. The most useful advice was from the woman who told me that she learned when her mother died that she should give herself a year to experience a whole cycle of events that would be significant – her mother's birthday, Mother's Day, her birthday without her mother, holidays that were important in their family.

Most of us have attended memorial or funeral services that didn't primarily reflect the life of the person who died. Yet, the memorial service for my mother was about my mother and the people in her life. It wasn't, as some funeral services I've experienced have been, a "fill in the blanks" service, not recognizing the individuality, the uniqueness of the person who died, not recognizing the unique relationship the deceased had with those in attendance at the service.

My father died in 2000. He died at home, in his sleep with his favorite radio station on. By the time my father died, I knew a lot about advance medical directives, and he had his paperwork all in order, but we didn't need it.

His memorial service was at the Brooklyn Society for Ethical Culture, the society where he was a member for most of his life, and where I grew up. The main meeting room of that Society, which is in an old mansion, has a ledge around it perhaps four feet up from the floor. My father was a photographer, and so I used the ledge to display photographs, mostly ones that he took, but some of him. The music was his favorite Hungarian gypsy music, and I even told his favorite joke about being Hungarian. My children participated. My son was the DJ, playing the music during the appropriate interludes. Again those assembled shared a sense of the person who my father was, no fill in the blanks service. My dad would have liked his memorial service too.

Humanists value and honor the uniqueness of each individual and our ceremonies reflect that value.

Humanist Memorials in Perspective

Memorial services offer an opportunity to celebrate a life and reflect on how our own lives were touched by the person who died. They can facilitate grieving. An Ethical Culture Leader, as Anne Klaeysen's chapter reflects, or some other trained officiant can be helpful in planning and/or presiding at a funeral or memorial service. There, however, is no legal necessity to have a licensed or certified officiant preside at a memorial service. Because death usually comes with great emotions, it can be especially helpful to have someone with experience in officiating at memorial services to at least assist in coordinating a service.

Funerals usually take place soon after death. Memorial services may be held at any time. A humanist officiant's comments will reflect the humanist values of caring, cooperation, and the uniqueness of each individual.

Whenever possible, family and friends meet with the officiant beforehand to discuss the nature and structure of the service. Suggestions for readings and music may be made. At the service, the officiant may deliver the eulogy or others present may do so.

A memorial service is a ceremony that makes us stop and pay attention to a change in our lives. It may be a major change if you were close to the person who died. If it is known that someone is dying, it is possible to have a living memorial service for her or him so that she or he can hear how much they have meant to the people whose lives they have touched. Such a service can be a joyous celebration of life. I like the way Alan Wolfelt, Director of the Center for Loss and Life Transition, sums up the purposes of a memorial service in his book *Creating Meaningful Funeral Ceremonies: A Guide for Caregivers.*[1] (As a rule, funeral services have the body of the person who died present, while memorial services do not. Yet they serve many of the same purposes.) His purposes for a memorial service correlate with humanist values:

- Acknowledge the reality of the death.
- Move toward the pain of the loss.
- Remember the person who died.
- Develop a new self-identity.
- Search for meaning.
- Receive ongoing support from others.

Humanists base their lives in reality. Acknowledging the reality of death, the pain of no longer having someone who was special in your life, searching for meaning and finding ways to have ongoing support in our lives are especially important for humanists. Because our beliefs are such that we do not expect to ever again have any direct interaction with the person who died, and because we do not have an instruction book or prescribed practices for what to do when someone dies, we need to figure it out. How we will accept the death of someone close to us? We need to ask ourselves what will we do to honor the person who died. Who are we without this person in our lives? Sometimes the very real question is, how will we keep living? Many humanists focus on human relationships. Once a person is dead, we need to form a new relationship with him or her. Just because someone isn't alive, doesn't mean they are no longer part of your life. Allow me to offer an example.

When I was about to have a certification ceremony as an Ethical Culture Leader, my mom had already been dead for ten years. I felt very sad that she would never know that I became an Ethical Culture Leader some 40 years after she first took me to Sunday School in Brooklyn. A friend said he was sure that somehow my mother knew. I said I didn't believe that and she wouldn't have believed it either. He meant to be comforting. What I did instead was to write letters to my mother, to think about my mother and to think about what she might have said to me if she were there, how proud and pleased she would have been. That practice allowed me to be more fully present on the day of the ceremony, rather than having my attention drawn away with sad thoughts about my mother. I had created a new identity for myself, not only as a Leader but as a person with a dead mother who would have been very proud of her.

1.   Alan D. Wolfelt, *Creating Meaningful Funeral Ceremonies: A Guide for Caregivers* (Fort Collins, CO: Companion Press, 1994).

Sometimes the remembrance isn't done collectively or formally, as at a memorial service. Sometimes people desire that there be no memorial service for them. If I happen to learn of such a wish, I try to have a conversation with them to ask why they don't want a service, and especially to explain that memorial services are not for the deceased. If there is no memorial service for someone who was important in your life, or you are not able to attend a service, you might want to find other ways to be intentional in acknowledging their death.

The idea of planning one's own memorial service, or obituary might seem very strange, macabre, or even have a sense of grandiosity. Yet this practice can serve several purposes. The primary one is that thinking about one's own death can enhance how we think about our lives. Thinking about what one hopes might be said at the time of one's death can provide motivation to live one's life as well as can be, to live as closely in accordance with one's values as possible. Planning your own memorial can also give guidance to those responsible for creating a memorial service for you. Of course, you can at best provide ideas and information; you won't be there.

In planning for my memorial service I gave some general instructions. They include that there be lots of music, with recommendations for specific pieces including John Lennon's "Imagine" and the Phil Ochs song "When I'm Gone." It has the message that you can't do anything after you die, so you need to do what you can while you are alive. Other requests are about flowers; like my mother, I don't much like carnations and if there are flowers they should be simple. Flowers grown in my garden would be ideal if I manage to die in-season. I request that people attending a memorial service for me be invited to speak about me, with a clear invitation that they are welcome to share the not so easy times they've had with me as well as all the wonderful, constructive, creative and fun times.

The reasoning for this last is that a humanist memorial service provides the opportunity to remember and reflect on a whole person. Often there is the impulse to say only wonderful things about the person who died. A memorial service isn't the place to fully air grievances or long-held grudges, but it might be a time to acknowledge challenges. As Ethical Culture Leader Algernon Black wrote in his book *Without Burnt Offerings,* "we would wish that those we love, those close in family and friendship, the neighbor and fellow worker, should understand what we lived for, our values and intentions, what we meant by our life at our best, seeing our faults and mistakes with understanding and generosity. We would want no eulogy or apology either."[2]

2.   Algernon Black, "Three Wishes at Death," in Black, *Without Burnt Offerings: Ceremonies of Humanism* (New York: The Viking Press, 1974).

While humanists tend to be accurate about the language they use for death and dying, the larger US society uses much language around death and dying that is either euphemistic or has religious meanings. To listen to or read the news media, or watch TV or movies, one might think that not many people die these days. It is reported that people have passed away, or perhaps passed. What have they passed – a life exam? In personal inter-actions you might hear that someone has passed over. To where have they passed over? There is the implication that they have "passed" into an after-life. This language is indicative of how many people do not want to face the fact that they will die, that we all will die. Using euphemistic language con-tributes to not accepting that dying, most times, is something that happens naturally, that is part of life.

There aren't rules for us to follow as humanists, no set of instructions for what to do when someone dies, although I hope what I offered above is useful food for thought. As always for humanists, it is up to us to select what practices and beliefs make sense to us. Sharing a death with others at a memorial service can be an important part of acknowledging this loss of life, helping you to keep living your life.

We don't know what happens after we die, so we must give our attention to living the life we know as best we can.

Section III:

On Acting like a Humanist

8 Politics and Political Life

Andrew Copson*

Before we begin to consider what the humanist worldview means for how we do politics and what we do politics for, we need briefly to rehearse what the humanist worldview is. In using the word "humanist" I mean one who accepts: that this natural universe we inhabit is one to which there is no parallel "supernatural" level; that the life we are living is the only life we will ever know and the individual human personality is annihilated at the moment of physical death; that the best way to get closest to truth is through free inquiry and applying reason to evidence. A humanist is one who believes that in the absence of any discernible purpose in the universe, we make meaning in our own lives in the here and now and that the end of morality is the welfare and happiness of human beings, now and in the future.

By applying the lens of biology to ourselves, we can see readily that what we call politics is a natural phenomenon that arises out of necessity: human beings are mutually dependent social animals living in groups and we need frameworks within which to make the group decisions that social existence requires. In understanding ourselves as products of natural processes on our small planet, rather than as players in a divinely ordained fantasia, we know

* Andrew Copson is Chief Executive of the British Humanist Association. His writing on humanist and secularist issues has appeared in *The Guardian*, *The Independent*, *The Times* and *New Statesman* as well as in various journals and he has represented the BHA and Humanism extensively on television news on BBC, ITV, Channel 4 and Sky, as well as on television programs such as *Newsnight*, *The Daily Politics*, *Sunday Morning Live* and *The Big Questions*. He has also appeared on radio programs from *Today*, *You and Yours*, *Sunday*, *The World Tonight*, *The World at One*, *The Last Word* and *Beyond Belief* on the BBC, to local and national commercial radio stations. He is a former director of the European Humanist Federation (EHF) and is currently First Vice-President of the International Humanist and Ethical Union (IHEU), where he leads on Communications. Andrew studied Classics and Ancient and Modern History at the University of Oxford.

these frameworks are not earthly reflections of some timeless cosmic order, but conscious human creations – elaborations on our social instincts that are to be made and unmade according to our needs.

It is on an explicit acknowledgement of these two facts – that its origin is as an aid to effective communal living and that it is the endeavour of men and women in the here and now – that a humanist politics must be built. The nature of what humanists will want to build on these foundations is conditioned by our values. In building it, we move beyond politics as a necessity towards politics as a virtue – the admirable craft by which we build a better world.

What's It All For?

If the origin of politics lies in the need for effective communal living then it could be seen as quite a minimal enterprise: the first purpose mere survival and the second some form of stability. We shouldn't denigrate these aims – for a great many of our ancestors they were the best that could be achieved and for too many members of the human family today they are still lacking. The right to life is still far from universal. At the same time, they are only the most basic purposes of social organization. It will seem to many of us that they are a poor minimum in a world where our technological accomplishments have scaled such heights and our culture evolved such rich diversity and depth. Perhaps a hierarchy of purposes might be the best way to approach a humanist view. If so, what might be the steps beyond survival and stability? There are a number of possibilities but all of the answers that a humanist can be expected to endorse fall under a single category: the development of the human person.[1]

If there is no life beyond the one we are now living, then we cannot look to any future state in which we might hope for fulfillment. Fulfillment – if it ever comes – must come in this life. We therefore obviously wish for ourselves the greatest possible personal development. The simple principle of treating others as we would wish to be treated in their position tells that this development that we seek for ourselves we should also wish for them. For a humanist these "others" will include not just friends, family, and members of our immediate tribe, but all members of the human family – and so we move rapidly from the personal into the political. I think a humanist view is that the happiness of its members – not just their security but also their

1.   For an example of just one attempt to formalize and measure this, see the Human Development Index and "capability approach" formulated by the humanist economist Amartya Sen and others. See http://hdr.undp.org/en.

good health, fulfillment in their relationships, their self-esteem, fulfillment in their employment, the high quality of their inner life – should be the aim of a community, once their safety is established. To the extent that politics is the means by which the community pursues its aims, the fulfillment of these things should be the aim of politics.

The first example we have of a society that tried to achieve such aims (with any historical record allowing us to judge it) is the ancient Greek city-state of Athens in its golden age. An early adopter of democratic principles, it offers a case study in what results when free people get together to decide on and then to consciously create a society and a politics for themselves. In 460–429 BCE Perikles was its leading citizen. He described the aspirations of Athens in these words, the gist of which, if not a verbatim account, is recorded for us by the historian Thucydides:[2]

> Our constitution does not imitate our neighbors', but acts as an example to them. We are called a democracy because government is in the hands of the many and not the few; but although there is indeed equal justice for all in their private disputes, the claims of excellence are also recognized. When a citizen has some particular talent, this is recognized in the role he is given in public life – not by privilege, but by merit. Poverty is not an obstacle to this – even the most deprived can be preferred...

> ...in our private lives we are not suspicious of one another, nor angry with our neighbor because he does what he likes; we do not look askance at him (which is not pleasant even if it doesn't do any harm). Although we are free in this way in our private lives, we suffuse our public acts with reverence; respect for the authorities and the law keeps us from doing the wrong thing and we hold in particular regard the laws that are in place to protect the wronged as well as the unwritten laws which bring public opprobrium on their violator...

> ...nor have we neglected to provide many relaxations from labor to refresh our spirits. We hold games and festivals throughout the year, our homes are elegant and attractive, and the pleasure we take every day in these things banishes sorrow...

> ... we alone do good for our neighbors not because we have cal-culated the advantages, but in the fullness of freedom in an open and courageous spirit.

2.   I can present only part of the speech here, but the whole will repay the time taken by anyone who reads it in full. It is found in Thucydides' *History of the Peloponnesian War* 2.34-46.

Today's humanists in many ways will have higher political standards than Perikles – we would not countenance slaves or the second-class treatment of women. But we can readily discern in his description of Athens a basic model of the sort of society we would aim for.[3]

Freedom

The first obvious distinguishing feature of this sort of society is freedom. The idea that one may do as one likes, as Perikles puts it, "in [one's] private business." The distinction between public and private is important here, because what is being talked about is not the freedom to do whatever one wants regardless of the effects on others. The humanistic framers of the 1789 *French Declaration of the Rights of Man and of the Citizen* understood this when they said that the rights of a person had "no limits except those that guarantee the enjoyment of the same rights to others." The British humanist John Stuart Mill in 1859 crystallized the principle as "The only purpose for which power can be rightfully exercised over any member of a civilized community, against his will, is to prevent harm to others." Any humanist politics will try to secure the maximum personal freedom that is compatible with the rights and freedoms of others.[4]

What is the point of this freedom? Mill, as I have suggested elsewhere, in the same *On Liberty* from which this famous principle is taken, provides a humanist answer.[5] He doesn't see himself as writing a handbook on politics but addressing the "the wellbeing of mankind" and his essay contains profound reflections on human flourishing that are a significant contribution to the humanist tradition. Mill's view is that, "Among the works of man, which human life is rightly employed in perfecting and beautifying, the first in importance surely is man himself."[6] Freedom is what offers the opportunity to engage in this employment unfettered. Mill encourages us to value not just experience, but also the discussion and examination of experience,

3.   To the extent that the humanist political philosopher Karl Popper used Perikles as his exemplar advocate of an open society in Popper *et al.*, *The Open Society and its Enemies* (New York: Routledge, 1945).

4.   John Stuart Mill, *On Liberty* (London: Longman, Roberts & Green Co., 1869; New York: Oxford University Press), p. 22.

5.   My discussion of Mill is drawn from "Face to Faith: We Should All Celebrate the 150th Anniversary of John Stuart Mill's On Liberty," *The Guardian*, October 30, 2009). See http://www.theguardian.com/commentisfree/belief/2009/oct/30/john-stuart-mill-on-liberty.

6.   Mill, *On Liberty*, p. 34.

so we can make our choices reflectively, developing "the human faculties of perception, judgment, discriminative feeling, mental activity, and...moral preference."[7] He encourages us to ask "what would allow the best and highest in me to have fair play, and enable it to grow and thrive?" so we can become "more valuable" to ourselves and "therefore capable of being more valuable to others." He believes that "human nature is not a machine...but a tree, which requires to grow and develop itself on all sides."[8] His clarion call is to begin work today on improving oneself and act always so as to guarantee for oneself and others the freedom that will enable this. Mill's own convictions about the worth and dignity of human life – vital principles for modern humanists – stimulated him in social action, opposition to slavery, and a commendably anachronistic appetite for gender equality.

When we believe, as humanists do, that the meaning of life is not singular but plural – that each one of us creates their own meaning – then freedom in this sphere is of course the only viable approach. We might in fact see it purely as a pragmatic necessity. But diversity of preferences of itself can also be a valid end, in that it is one of the things that make the world more colourful and interactions with other people more fascinating. Life would be pretty boring if we were all the same. One of the very many reasons why I am happier to live in London than I would be to live in Riyadh today, or Moscow 30 years ago, would be what I perceive to be the "dullness" of such places. Closed or totalitarian societies, where conformity and uniformity are what is striven for, are the sort of societies that humanists reject and fight against, not just because of the lack of freedom for the individual, but also because of the concomitant crushing of the exuberant diversity that makes humanity so enjoyable a family of which to be a part.

Equality

An important second feature of the good society is social solidarity. Some aspiration of this sort is present in almost all societies – note how Perikles praises in particular the Athenian laws that operate to make more secure the position of the most unfortunate – but it finds its fullest expression to date in the systems of social security of modern societies. Such provision obviously includes health services, housing, and some guarantee of economic means, but in many states the guarantee has gone or does go much further, extending to employment, lifelong education, old-age care, or high relative levels of income. Equality is a slippery and ambiguous concept, but in all cases what

7.   Mill, *On Liberty*, p. 34.
8.   Mill, *On Liberty*, p. 34.

can definitely be said is that these systems aim to reduce *inequalities* between individuals on certain grounds. Inasmuch as they arise out of the desire to secure for every person the highest standard of life possible, they can be said to be humanist.

Even the word "inequality" always needs to be qualified because, although human beings certainly have much in common as human beings, we will never be equal in the sense of being identical in every aspect. An obvious inequality is the economic – and that is an inequality that is unfortunately probably greater now than it has ever been in human history. But, apart from economic inequality, there is a wide range of grounds on which people experience inequalities within our world and our local societies. Differential treatment based on sex, sexual orientation, ethnicity, religion and ideology or belief, physical ability, social class, skin color, and nationality – especially in areas of life that are fundamental, like access to education or privacy – is still widespread, though declining. Humanists will want to move as near to eliminating it entirely as possible so as to maximize opportunities for all and many humanists have led the way in doing so.[9] This is really just an extension of the desire to expand individual freedom: it is a constraint on the individual to have their personal autonomy limited by factors out of their control like economic condition or skin color, and it is just of us to limit the damage to individual potential that such accidents can wreak. The increasing evidence that inequality within a society has a negative impact on happiness across the whole of that society – including for the people at the top of the pile[10] – adds an extra dimension to the argument by adding an empirical element to the emotional reaction that many of us have to inequality, feeling that it diminishes us as persons metaphorically.

9.   It is no coincidence that the authors of the three pivotal texts of modern feminism – Mary Wollstonecraft, *A Vindication of the Rights of Women* (Boston: Peter Edes, 1792), John Stuart Mill, *The Subjection of Women* (London: Longmans, Green, Readers & Dyer, 1869), and Simone de Beauvoir, *The Second Sex* (New York: Random House, 1949) – were all humanists. Many pioneering women politicians, such as Lady Wootton, the first appointed female member of the House of Lords in the UK, have also been humanists.

10. See, for example, Richard Wilkinson and Kate Pickett, *The Spirit Level: Why equality is Better for Everyone* (New York: Penguin, 2010), at least one author of which – Kate Pickett – is herself a humanist.

Fulfillment

Freedom and equality are the social conditions in which widespread personal development is most likely to be realized but there are a number of ways in which the good state facilitates personal development much more directly. Athens' provision of games, festivals, and beautiful things to be enjoyed – as well as the encouragement of education – find their analogues throughout the ages and all over the world wherever free men and women put their heads together to build a good society. The humanist and socialist Clement Attlee, Prime Minister of the UK from 1945 to 1951, was never so eloquent as when he was describing the libraries and galleries in which he hoped the working classes, liberated from squalor, ignorance and want by the welfare state, would find their fulfillment. Whether it is the public funding of sports facilities, scientific research, museums, galleries, schools, institutes of higher education, parks, and so on, the state informed by humanistic principles takes action to secure not just the freedom and social security of its citizens, but opportunities for their expanding capacity to live the good life, have fun, and grow as persons.

Politics can be the vehicle for securing for a larger number of people than would otherwise be possible the best things that everyone desires for themselves and others in this life. Where that is the aim, the enterprise is surely a humanist one.

It's the Way That You Do It

Politics is a process and there are more and less humanist ways of carrying it on, just as there are more and less humanist aims for it. In fact the aims of politics and the way it is carried out are in many ways interdependent. Looking back at the words of Perikles we can see immediately that, inextricably interwoven with his account of what sort of society and people the Athenians are, is an account of the way in which they do politics – the authority that underpins their constitution, the way in which decisions are made, and so on.

Obedience to an unquestionable authority as a way of conducting political life is not likely to satisfy any humanist – one who, as we have said, puts reason first, and values evidence, clear-thinking, and open debate in the search for truth. To a humanist, a deliberative politics, informed by the best knowledge, is going to be essential. Equally essential will be an acceptance that no political order can be god-given, and no one founding father a timeless authority. Authority must come from some other source. Given that a humanist ethic prizes reciprocity, ample scope for participation by each person is also going to be essential. We all want some say in how our common life is to be run, and so we should extend that same ability to others.

As a result of all this, some form of democracy has got to be the most attractive political order. At the same time, history shows that total democracy with no holds barred can lead to mob rule and the potential for terrible violations of human dignity and individual freedom. Some check on the potential excesses of popular authority must be equally crucial in any political system advanced as in keeping with humanism. Given that no source of authority outside humanity can be pleaded, the quest is to set the origin of authority as far beyond the arbitrary say-so of any one individual human as possible. Instead, we seek to have it reflect the general aspirations of humanity on the grounds that, if objective moral truth exists anywhere, it is within the collective experience of humanity as a whole. Law is the concept that results, as a source of authority itself in the idea of "the rule of law" and as a pragmatic limit to total democracy. Law manifests itself through systems of judiciary that apply fair rules impartially, constitutions framed to enshrine the highest principles, and mechanisms of accountability on those entrusted with power by the community. It finds perhaps its highest expression in the human rights instruments that are a feature of the last century or so.

The rule of law, democracy and human rights, underpinned as they are by the equality of every person in the face of justice, the equal right of every person to a say in the decision-making processes, and the aspiration of a minimum standard of treatment that every person can be guaranteed, seem to be the essential building blocks of a political order a humanist could support. To operate, they require freedom of thought and speech; none of them can exist where individuals are banned from speaking or fear to speak their mind, where opinions cannot be circulated and propounded freely, or where opposition to established or majority views is proscribed. They are also mutually balancing concepts, and no one of them stands alone. For the sake of understanding them better, however, let's examine them separately.

Human rights

"…recognition of the inherent dignity and of the equal and inalienable rights of all members of the human family is the foundation of freedom, justice and peace in the world…"[11] Rights are expressed in many forms in many different societies but I take as my text here the Universal Declaration

---

11.   This quotation is from the preamble of the Universal Declaration of Human Rights, adopted and proclaimed by the General Assembly of the United Nations, December 10, 1948.

of Human Rights because of its historical significance and the beauty of its prose, but also because what is true of it is true of rights instruments generally. In spite of the fact that human rights have been called "values for a godless age"[12] and humanists such as John Boyd Orr, Brock Chisholm, and Julian Huxley[13] were immediately prominent in putting the sentiments of the UN Declaration into practice, some question whether a morality that does not hold to a source of moral authority over and above humanity can ever convincingly underwrite such sentiments of inherent human worth as in the preamble quoted above. In fact, a humanist foundation of universal human rights and human dignity is easily identified.

We start by frankly admitting that there is no such thing as a "natural" right. All rights that have ever been enshrined in any declaration or upheld at any tribunal are human creations sustained by the will of human societies. They are sustained by the will of humanity generally and specifically by the political and judicial systems that we have established. How do we as individuals wish to be treated? The answer to this question is what provides humanists with the principles that guide their treatment of others. How would we in the situation of the other wish to be treated? On a global scale, the answers provide us with the foundation of human rights. No one wishes to be coerced, so the coercion of another is wrong, and no one should seek to coerce another. Indeed, the development of the Declaration is a microcosm of how humanists see morality as originating. Just as the need to live together in communities made humanity inclined to the sort of behaviour that facilitates communal life; the development of human rights as a set of entitlements for all flowed from the mid-twentieth century need to prevent the recurrence of the terrible suffering and misery that we inflicted on each other in the opening decades of that century.

In today's world the extension of rights to all of humanity makes sense in terms of self-interest. Indeed, in our Universal Declaration, though we make claims for the inherent dignity of man, we are also up-front about the pragmatic motivations for these claims. As motivations for the Declaration, are given that "disregard and contempt for human rights have resulted in barbarous acts which have outraged the conscience of mankind," that "it is essential, if man is not to be compelled to have recourse, as a last resort, to rebellion against tyranny and oppression, that human rights should be protected by the rule of law," and that "it is essential to promote the development of friendly relations between nations." All in all, there is a heavy

12.   Francesca Klug, *Values for a Godless Age* (London: Penguin, 2000).
13.   The first Directors-General of the UN Food and Agricultural Organisation, World Health Organisation, and UNESCO respectively.

dose of pragmatism at the root of the Declaration, side by side with all its elevated language of dignity, worth and inherent equality. Most humanists would not think that these two features of are incompatible. Why should recognition of the pragmatic foundation of the rights somehow diminish them or render them inert? The humanists Jeremy Bentham and John Stuart Mill did not believe that rights were "natural" yet they both had a deep hatred of slavery and arbitrary coercion.

Is it not in fact a source of great wonder that mankind, scattered and divided in nations, ideologies and tribes around the world, came together to agree these principles, and in the wake of violent wars and genocides, recognized that peace was a great end and that, to reach it, a global culture of reciprocity and respect was essential? Many humanists would say it was, and that we do not necessarily need to explicate the foundations of these rights beyond an understanding of the historical and present-day contexts that make them essential. We could commit to upholding them simply on that basis.

Nonetheless, behind the particulars of our great modern legal instruments of human rights *do* sit assumptions of the inherent worth of each human being. Article 1 of the Declaration asserts that "All human beings are born free and equal in dignity and rights." For a humanist, can there be such inherent worth? Well, the ties that create a unity of mankind and support the concept of inherent worth certainly cannot derive from the fact of a single creation; when humanists seek knowledge about the biological nature of man, they seek them from biologists, not sacred texts. But the biological relationship that exists in fact between every human being can be the foundation of a wider application of the golden rule: recognition of the human race as one. An acknowledgment of our common nature as present living humans, born of shared, though distant, ancestors can give the foundation for an extension of the golden rule to all humanity. Such a one was humanist author and scientist Charles Darwin, who in *The Descent of Man* in 1871 expressed his view that,

> As man advances in civilisation, and small tribes are united into larger communities, the simplest reason would tell each individual that he ought to extend his social instincts and sympathies to all the members of the same nation, though personally unknown to him. This point being once reached, there is only an artificial barrier to prevent his sympathies extending to the men of all nations and races.[14]

14.   Charles Darwin, *The Descent of Man* (London: John Murray, 1871), pp. 100–101.

We can see our own humanity in the other's face, and the Declaration is a great affirmation of the view that there are important moral values shared by all rational people, regardless of race, culture or religion, because they are based on our shared human nature and needs. That there are such values, and that they can be guaranteed by humanity itself through the law and not by the stamp of any other authority is a central humanist political claim.

The rule of law

We have already spoken of law as being a source of authority that, for humanists, will do at least one of the jobs that god does for religious political systems. The role of the law is as an essential check on the potential arbitrariness of those in power, whether monarch or people. Equal treatment before the law for every person is of course an absolute requirement in this context. Gods may have their favourites, but the law must not. And instead of stemming from individual men in the way that law made by a monarch does, and in the absence of any other source of authority outside of humanity generally, humanity must be the source of the law.

This idea has antecedents in ancient Roman thought but is best crystallized now in a political theory called "social contract theory." The most amenable version of the theory for humanists will be that of John Rawls in his *Theory of Justice*. He hypothesized an "original position" wherein the members of a society stand behind a "veil of ignorance," where they are ignorant of the situation, skills, and condition they will have in their society, and ask themselves in the abstract what sort of order they would like to obtain. Being reasonable, they would choose a society where justice for all was the guiding principle. This is a good thought experiment to bring home to each person the need for justice, of which the rule of law is a part. But whence does the law come in reality? It is, of course, the accretion of principles for good living over time, adjusted by society as necessary. We should recognize this and humanists will not shy away from the fact that laws – even big laws – are and should be subject to change with changing circumstances. If a law has obtained for centuries that thieves ought to be imprisoned on the grounds that a good short sharp shock of deprivation will prevent them committing further crimes in the future, but the evidence of centuries shows that it is not imprisonment which prevents recidivism but restorative justice and education, then it is not acceptable for us to insist on the maintenance of the imprisonment law in the face of such evidence. The law must change.

The foundation for law cannot, of course, be all of the people all of the time. We cannot endlessly revisit all our laws every generation but the law will change with new facts and the social consensus. To be effective, new thinking, dissent and advancing of new facts by individuals must have an outlet, and with this in mind we come to democracy.

Democracy

The idea that men and women should have a say in the government of their society is not predominant in human history. Even in most societies that have developed participatory political systems at least one half of the populations have been disenfranchised from the start on account of their sex. Even a sizeable minority, and sometimes a majority, of the adult male population have often also been excluded. Many societies have had forms of slavery that have excluded substantial numbers from participation. Less severe forms of property qualification have served as a further economic barrier to enfranchisement. In other cases, restrictions of age, ethnicity, nationality, and mental impairment have applied – and still do apply. A humanist approach will tend to favour participation of all the members of society in society's decisions for reasons of reciprocal morality and mutual respect. That democracy – if we value evidence and reason – should be deliberative rather than just rely on the results of snap votes. A humanist approach will also tend to favour political equality. We do not need to agree entirely with the American humanist William James that truth is founded in what works for each individual person to nonetheless accept that every person has a claim to know something of the truth. It follows that, if any voice is subjugated or silenced, it is the community as a whole that loses out, not just the individual.

Of course, some restrictions on enfranchisement do make sense. We will want to exclude from participation those who are so mentally impaired that they cannot make informed decisions, we will want to exclude all those who do not have sufficient maturity as yet to make decisions, and we want to exclude those who are not really part of the community – people who are just passing through, or present temporarily. The more we think about all this, however, the less easy it seems than at first glance. The case for a single age at which maturity is deemed to be sufficient is surely inadequate, for example. Individuals reach maturity at different times – we all know 14-year olds with greater maturity than some 20-year olds. Why should the latter be enfranchised and not the former? And it is surely not the case that one becomes suddenly mature enough all at once to make all decisions? Surely there are sorts of decision that 14-year olds are capable to make in relation to some areas of policy and public life? And is every form of mental impairment that is currently thought to rule one out truly an absolute barrier? Is it not possible to discern some preferences even when people are not capable of articulating them fully? If we were serious about the right of each person to the maximum extent possible, ought we not go to greater lengths to facilitate that? If we take democracy seriously, we need to be taking seriously the answers to these and many other questions of enfranchisement, not least the question of its relevance at all in an age of corporate power. If we do so and whenever we step back and look at any sort of government – whether local, national, or on an even smaller level than that, within public or quasi-public institutions – we can almost always see how they could be made more democratic, more participatory.

This is even truer when we start to think globally. We live in a world where communities are increasingly interconnected and interdependent. Five hundred years ago, it did not really matter to my ancestors what decisions were made by the government of China; today it matters to me very much and may matter to my descendants a whole lot more. If we take democratic principles seriously, nation states begin to look anachronistic in such a world. It would undoubtedly be a more democratic world if government were global, and just because the achievement of such a situation would be hard-fought is no reason not to work for that end. Greater progress towards it will have to come in the decades and centuries ahead if humanity is to live democratically, and perhaps even survive.

I've avoided here any discussion of the different forms of democracy and all questions of structure. That isn't because they're not important, nor because there is nothing to distinguish between parliamentary and direct democracies or the selection of legislators by lot and the selection of legislators by voting. But the question of which form is better is an empirical question, and I mainly want here to state and endorse the democratic principle – the idea that individuals should have the right to participate in the act of making decisions that affect society.

Secularism

It may seem surprising that I have not headlined the political principle of secularism before now, since it is undoubtedly the political principle which in societies traditionally dominated by the religions of Islam and Christianity has been hardest fought by humanists historically. There are two reasons why I have not mentioned it until now. One is because it is quite a culturally specific idea and I have tried to be more universal than that in discussing concepts. The second, however, is that I believe that secularism is largely constituted by the political features which I have set out – democracy, human rights, and the rule of law, underwritten by freedom of thought and speech. Non-secular states are ones in which religious institutions have the power to subvert democracy, or stand outside the rule of law, or opt-out of human rights, or limit the freedom of men and women to speak their minds or think freely. States in which democracy, human rights, and the rule of law obtain, I believe, will be secular perforce.[15]

Individuals Engaging in Society

In order to have a participatory politics, we must have citizens capable of participation: a democratic society is only sustained by men and women of a democratic character. What is this character? Clearly, we want our citizens to be critical thinkers, to be rational: they must have the capacity to weigh up matters and arrive at an opinion based on balanced consideration of the arguments rather than sentiment and prejudice. We will want them to be compassionate. My political actions affect you and yours affect me. How you vote will decide whether I am to be housed if homeless or helped if unemployed, taxed or benefited. I must be able to trust you to be sympathetic to your fellow citizens when you vote or exercise any other of your political powers. We will want our citizens to be free in thought, with a sense of their responsibility to society as well as the proportionate self-worth that enables such a feeling of obligation. None of us are finished articles, for our whole lives we are the developing products of our own responsible undertaking, but we could certainly do a better job of educating young people in schools in particular in the skills required of citizens, and put them on a better track towards a democratic path than we do currently. We must not reduce human beings to merely components of society, but given the challenges we face and the inherent fragility of democracy and of the wide political order we have admired, I think there is a strong case for suffusing all education with this aim, both in schools and otherwise.[16]

Because the prospect of a humanist world as I have described it – a good society based on freedom, social justice and individual development; a politics based on open democratic processes, the rule of law, and human rights – really does face serious threats today. Huge socio-economic inequalities globally and within nations; the turbulent unreason of ideology – economic, political or religious; the dehumanizing distance that complicated bureaucracies put

15.   There is, of course, much more to be said about secularism. Richard Norman's edited volume, *The Case for Secularism: A Neutral State in an Open Society* (London: British Humanist Association, 2007) says it very well.

16.   As with every other topic I have touched on here, there is much more to be said. Any of the work of the late Sir Bernard Crick – lifelong humanist, distinguished political scientist and pioneer of UK Citizenship Education – would be a good place for an interested reader to begin.

between people: these are just a few of them. Predictable and unpredictable future challenges guarantee we will never live in a utopia: not in this world, and never in any other place. But a progressive improvement in the condition of humanity is possible and every one of us can play our part in that task. In doing so we keep faith with the past – the countless generations of men and women who sustained our scattered human communities and brought us to this point. We can also provide a model to the future, always ensuring that our actions in building that better world are true to the highest ideals of the common good. Such a politics is a noble enterprise, and a humanist one in form and aspiration.

9   From a Human-Centered to a Life-Centered Humanism

Henk Manschot* and Caroline Šuranský**

An Urgent Global Problem

The past century has seen much progress in terms of human development. The United Nations Development Program (UNDP)'s human development indicators show global progress, from life expectancy to per capita income to education. Good news indeed, but this progress also brought us new causes for

*   Henk Manschot, a member of the University for Humanist Studies faculty, is co-founder and Director of Kosmopolis, the Humanist Institute for Global Ethics and World Citizenship of the University for Humanistics in Utrecht, the Netherlands. Kosmopolis is dedicated to engaging in interdisciplinary research, teaching, training and networking and seeks to link questions of personal meaning and spirituality with social and political issues of human and sustainable development worldwide. His current research focuses on interconnections between human and sustainable development and on cosmo-political education. He is Vice-Chairman/Secretary of the Asia-Europe Foundation CE-DESD and Head of the sector Dialogues, Leadership and Values. He is also Chairman of the Encounter of World Views Foundation. Manschot is a Graduate of the Sorbonne University in Paris, and he received his PhD from the Department of Philosophy of the University of Groningen in the Netherlands.

** Caroline Šuranský is on faculty at the University for Humanist Studies (Utrecht). She studied philosophy of education at the University of Utrecht and the University of Michigan in Ann Arbor. In 1998 she was awarded a grant to study the historical and political education ties between the Netherlands and South Africa at the University of Durban-Westville in South Africa. She worked from 1988 to 1998 at the same university as a lecturer in Curriculum Studies and coordinator of the Master's program in "Teacher Education." She is a Fellow of Cosmopolis (Humanist Institute for Global Ethics and World Citizenship) and co-founder and co-coordinator of the annual Summer School on Human Development and Human Rights, an initiative in collaboration with the Humanist Institute for Development Cooperation (HIVOS).

concern because, during the same period, human impact on the natural world has greatly intensified. The gains in human wellbeing present us with new global problems. More human wellbeing has meant more demand for energy, food, water and other resources. This problem has not stayed unnoticed.

Over the last decades, the international community has become increasingly aware of the ecological problems in the world. Numerous international as well as local organizations have investigated the situation and expressed their concerns, often backed by alarming statistics. Through its Environmental Program, the United Nations focuses on a wide array of issues, including climate change, eco-disasters and dealing with harmful substances. The Global Footprint Network[1] states that humanity, as a collective, currently uses the equivalent of 1.5 planets to provide the resources people across the world use, as well as to absorb the resulting waste. This means that it currently takes the Earth one year and six months to regenerate what human beings use in a year. The Earth's resources turn into waste faster than people can turn back their waste into resources again. In short, this means we deplete the very resources on which humanity and all biodiversity depend. UN scenarios suggest that if the current population and consumption trends continue, by the 2030s, we will need the equivalent of two Earths to support us. It raises the question: do we human beings still fit on the planet? However, since we only have one planet the question should probably be: what will it take for humanity to live within the means of one planet?

In order to recognize the ecological limits of the Earth, human beings are challenged to find new ways to live in sustainable ways within the Earth's possibilities. But that is easier said than done.

One of the problems is that, although environmental problems are clearly global problems, we need to deal with major differences across the world when we want to address human development concerns within the context of the ecological limitations of the Earth. There are immense global inequalities in terms of access of different nations and their communities to the Earth's resources. The fast growing economies of India and China, for instance, demand access to natural resources similar in scope and ways that bring the modern Western world much of its welfare. Hence, they are currently engaged in vast dam-building projects in the Himalayas as they seek new sources of energy to power their economies and supply their growing urban areas with electricity. Many of the proposed dams would be among the tallest in the world, able to generate more than 4000 megawatts, as much as the Hoover Dam on the Colorado River in the United States.[2]

1. http://www.footprintnetwork.org.
2. See John Vidal, in "China and India 'Water Grab' Dams Put Ecology of

Would it be fair for the developed Western world to deny the developing nations their economic growth and progress in the realm of human development? Understandably, a growing number of developing nations in the "global South" point out that the collective footprint of the Western world is the chief cause of the Earth's ecological problems and that these nations should bear the primary responsibility to address the problematic situation, while they catch up and work on the alleviation of poverty.

The situation is indeed complex and while international institutions, such as the United Nations, do much to raise global consciousness about environmental concerns, they lack the political power to intervene in national affairs and policies that could redress the situation. The incompatibility of the Human Development Index figures and the statistics on humanity's ecological footprint makes clear that we need to rethink our concept of human wellbeing. Currently, the more human development we achieve, the more detrimental it is for life on Earth. We therefore believe it is necessary to rethink our understanding of "development," human dignity and human well-being in relationship to the Earth.

In this chapter, we argue the current ecological crisis is foremost a crisis of values.[3] In order to address this crisis, we suggest worldviews, both religious and non-religious, including humanism, help us understand the emergence of the crisis, as well as being a value basis by means of which to redress the situation.

We briefly delve into the history of humanism and conclude that humanists roots within the Renaissance, Enlightenment and Modernity offer an explanation as to why humanists seem to have neglected to respond in the name of humanism to the global ecological crisis. Subsequently, we will advocate a shift from a human-centered to a life-centered humanist worldview and we explore new possibilities for knowledge, passion and action as three dimensions of this shift.

A Crisis of Values

The ways we currently try to achieve human development and a dignified life for all human beings is irreconcilable with the ecological possibilities of

Himalayas in Danger," posted on the Guardian's Alpha website. http://www.theguardian.com/global-development/2013/aug/10/china-india-water-grab-dams-himalayas-danger.

3.   Parts of this chapter are adaptations from an earlier publication (in Dutch) by Henk Manschot. "Over ecologisch (wereld)burgerschap en de toekomst van het hedendaags humanism," *Tijdschrift voor Humanistiek* 29, 2007.

the Earth. This problem can be examined from scientific, social, political and also spiritual perspectives. Therefore, some stress economic factors and point to economic inequalities; others emphasize political factors and try to fuel a sense of political urgency; still others point to the need for new and innovative green technologies. A wide diversity of perspectives is indeed valuable and needed to analyze and address the ecological problems on Earth.

Again, we advance the idea that the ecological crisis is, above all, a *crisis of values*. We believe the current situation certainly requires economic, political and technological changes, but it is critically important to reflect upon the values that have guided human behavior and played a major role in our pathways to the current ecological crisis. If one holds to the idea that the global ecological crisis is foremost a crisis of values, it seems sensible to turn to key sources of values – namely worldviews. Both religious and other worldviews, including humanism, are important sources of meaning to human beings. Worldviews offer meaning frames to people that help them to develop their key norms and values, beliefs, convictions and behavior. Worldviews also help many people to experience deeper existential meaning in their lives and offer them a basis for their internal moral compass. World-views are important shapers of culture. It could be helpful to reflect on the value frameworks of religious and other worldviews to help us understand not only the emergence of the current crisis of values but also to address it.

The Yale-based professors Mary Evelyn Tucker and John Grim do exactly that. They dedicate much of their academic life to studying the relationship between religious (and a number of non-religious) worldviews and ecology. In their work, they not only focus on the major world religions, such as Christianity or Islam, but also include other worldviews such as Taoism and indigenous traditions. They believe a wide diversity of worldviews can and should be more actively involved with the development of a new, more comprehensive worldview and ethics to ground all kinds of movements toward sustainability. They argue, "the attitudes and values that shape people's concepts of nature come primarily from religious worldviews and ethical practices." They even suggest, "moral imperative and value systems of religions are indispensable in mobilizing the sensibilities of people toward preserving the environment for future generations."[4] In the words of Tucker and Grim: "Religions have developed ethics for homicide, suicide, and genocide; now their challenge is to encompass biocide and ecocide."[5]

4.   See overview of Mary Evelyn Tucker and John Grim's *The Religions of the World and Ecology Book Series* at http://fore.research.yale.edu/publications/books/cswr/.

5.   Tucker and Grim, *Religions of the World and Ecology.*

In the 1990s, they brought together numerous scholars, religious leaders, spiritual leaders, and environmental activists who generated a substantial body of literature on how nature is valued in the world's various religious systems and worldview systems. They also organized ten conferences that came to a conclusion at the United Nations. One of the results of these efforts was an impressive book series[6] in which the relationship with nature and ecology of many of the world's major religious traditions and non-religious worldviews is explored. More recently, they have completed their work on the *Journey of the Universe* film, book, and educational DVD series.[7] Their initiative is the largest international project of its kind.

When we reflect on these important efforts, we discover that humanism is painfully absent. In the above-mentioned book series, we find titles such as *Islam and Ecology*, *Buddhism and Ecology* and *Indigenous Traditions and Ecology*, but there is no volume on humanism and ecology. This is an issue: we argue humanism has much to offer to critical reflection on the underlying causes of the current crisis of values and we believe humanism can and should contribute to the development of a new value framework for sustainable living.

Humanism and Ecology: A Blind Spot?

A few years ago, at a Conference of European Humanists, we asked the audience, "What do you consider the most impressive event on ecology and sustainable development organized by humanists in the last five years?" A long and uncomfortable silence followed.

This exchange tangibly suggests that humanists may have neglected to respond to the global ecological crisis in the name of humanism. It seems people experience humanism and ecology as two separate and unconnected worlds. There certainly are many humanists who are highly conscious of the ecological crisis and who are dedicated to living a green lifestyle. They may buy organic food, they may have installed solar panels on their roof and drive a hybrid car, but they do not associate these life choices with their humanist worldview. Why not? Let us explore some possible reasons by briefly reflecting on the history of humanism.

Humanism does not allow itself to be easily defined within a cultural and philosophical spectrum. Unlike most other world religions and ideologies,

6.   Tucker and Grim, eds. *Religions of the World and Ecology Book Series*, http://fore.research.yale.edu/publications/books/cswr/.

7.   http://www.journeyoftheuniverse.org.

there is no collective corpus of texts unequivocally canonized as belonging to the "tradition of humanism." It, however, can be stated that humanism has consistently defined itself with claims that humanity should be the starting point and foundation for the attribution of meaning in life. Humanism thus elevated humanity and inspired human beings to understand themselves as "the measure of all things." By taking this principle as its main point of departure, humanism distinguishes itself from other world views which start from different foundations and adhere to other fundamental doctrines, such as the transcendental God in monotheist religions; "Nature as Process" in Taoism and the interaction between Heaven and Earth in Confucianism.

The European Renaissance (fourteenth-sixteenth centuries) played a crucial part in the development of humanism. This is because the identification of humankind as the foundation of meaning draws on a biblical view of humankind developed in the Renaissance. Humankind is not only presented as created by God, but rather created "in the image and likeness of God." These words were subsequently interpreted as an assignment, a human task to become *Imago Dei*, or the mirror image of God. In the course of the Renaissance and the following centuries, this task was taken more and more literally. Qualities that were previously exclusively attributed to God, such as transcendence, or God's roles as Creator and Legislator, were gradually assigned to human beings. Through the identification to such divine attributes, human beings gradually saw themselves as the main source and foundation of their own existence. In a process of secularization, humanists saw God progressively recede to the background. During the Enlightenment (eighteenth century) this "immanent transcendentalization"[8] was proclaimed the basis of the moral autonomy of humanity. It is easy to understand why this "Enlightenment mentality" gave a tremendous impulse to the growth of modern humanism. The proclamation of autonomy, freedom, equality and the intrinsic dignity of all human beings served to develop some of the basic intuitions of a humanist doctrine for all essential human relationships: with the world, with other people and with the self. The principle of (human) transcendence itself, previously described as one of the pillars of the Enlightenment, became increasingly vital to the image of modern humanism. Up until today, humanism and the Enlightenment have been closely associated.

The central premises and values of humanism, namely freedom and equality, intrinsic human dignity, the rule of law and democracy still are some of the most fundamental values in humane societies. We believe humanism

8.   This term is attributed to Jean-Marie Schaeffer, who discusses this development in his book, *La fin de l'exception humaine* (Paris: Gallimard, 2007).

significantly contributes to the idea that all human beings have intrinsic value that they are an end in and of themselves. However, the ecological crisis also made us realize an exclusive focus on the wellbeing and dignity of human beings comes with limitations. In its principal focus on human beings, humanism seems to have neglected its relationship with nature. Is this a blind spot?

In order to address this question, we turn to the relationship between humanism and modernity because we think that the origins of this blind spot are deeply rooted within the culture and the values of modernity. The history of modernity is construed in many ways, but is mainly aligned with the age of Enlightenment, also known as the Age of Reason.

An important point of departure for the culture and values of modernity is revealed in two of its basic principles or theoretical prisms. Firstly, modernity assumes a radical dichotomy between the value of human beings and the value of other organisms. Secondly, modernity meant that technological – and instrumentalist – attitudes toward non-human life forms were considered adequate. This attitude elevated humans above all other living beings and rendered them autonomous, capable of assigning form and content to their own existence. Human acts were thus radically distinguishable from "natural processes." While nature was subjected to natural processes, human beings were able to transcend these processes and thus become masters of their own destiny.

Many philosophers and scientists have argued that there is an intrinsic link between modernity and blindness towards nature. Much ecologically inspired criticism of modernity affirms that modern culture has been the foundation of the attitude to strive to exercise human control over life and subordinate nature to humankind. This "Enlightenment mentality" seems double-faced. On the one hand, one can argue that it is one of the most dynamic and transforming ideologies in the history of humankind.[9] To a great extent, the Enlightenment and modernity meant that people began to consider humane living conditions as an essential constituent of a dignified human life. Many of these standards of humaneness have since been declared as inalienable universal human rights. But with globalization and the expansion of western modern lifestyles, we also discovered the dark sides of this pattern. This made us more aware of the unforeseen destructive side effects of modern lifestyles on the planet's ecosystems. Our earlier reference to the incompatibility of human development standards and Footprint measurements make these destructive sides evident.

9.   Tu Weiming, "The Ecological Turn in New Confucian Humanism," in Tu Weiming and Mary Evelyn Tucker, eds, *Confucian Spirituality: Volume Two* (New York: The Crossroads Publishing Company, 2004).

The central quest for dignity for all human beings meant the intrinsic value of other living beings remained underrated. Human beings assumed they had a moral right to use and manipulate other living beings and the Earth's natural resources to further their own wellbeing and happiness. At first, the scale at which this happened did not lead to major disturbances of the main life patterns on the planet, but in the last half century new mass industrial and technological developments demanded more and more from the Earth. Currently we are in a situation in which human behavior impacts all planetary developments. Or as Paul Hawken argues: "For better and for worse, we now occupy a human planet, one in which most evolutionary forces are guided or misguided by our hand... Human agency will alter the fate of all living beings because no part of the planet is unaffected by our activities."[10]

The ecological crisis presents human beings with the need to develop a new value – and knowledge framework – which will allow us to achieve human wellbeing while at the same time secure the wellbeing of the much broader community of life. This new framework should not take the mere continued existence of humanity as a basic point of departure, but life on Earth in a much broader sense. This means valuing life on Earth, which includes human life, but doing so without separating human beings from the broader community of life. Humanism, as an important source of value for people across the globe, could positively contribute to the development of a new value and knowledge framework that connects human life to the larger biosphere. But, a radical re-orientation within humanism may be essential.

We believe humanism's current core values are neither obsolete nor should they be abandoned. Rather they need to be re-considered and re-imagined from the perspective of the greater community of life. Tu Weiming called this more inclusive perspective as a shift from an anthropo*centric* to an anthropo*cosmic* worldview. His ideas express a conviction that the centrality of universal human dignity and wellbeing should not be abandoned, but that that these principles need to be contextualized in the broader perspective of the cosmos. He writes: "Not man, but life of the terrestrial community as a whole, aimed at a shared future, should become the coordinating framework." The values of *life, liberty and the pursuit of happiness* that comprise a summary of the *Enlightenment mentality*, take on a new form here.[11]

10.   Paul Hawken, *Blessed Unrest: How the Largest Movement in the World Came Into Being, and Why No One Saw It Coming* (New York: Viking Penguin, 2007), p. 12. In many of his articles and books, Hawken defends the thesis that human beings now have the capacity to actively alter the fate of all living beings due to their impact on the Earth.

11.   Weiming, "The Ecological Turn in New Confucian Humanism," pp. 480–507. See also, Tu Weiming, "The Continuity of Being: Chinese Visions of

From a *Human*-Centered to a *Life*-Centered Humanist Worldview

Since Darwin proclaimed his evolution theory in the nineteenth century, many scientific disciplines have developed new ideas about the creation of the universe. The more we know about the history of the Earth, the more we begin to realize that humankind is only a latecomer in a staggering play of evolutionary powers. Life on Earth clearly came into being independently of humankind. If we also take into consideration the periodization of the evolutionary process, we see that human beings only appeared towards the very end of the last period. This period, in which mammals evolved, is estimated to have begun some 65 million years ago. Contemporary scientific discoveries keep revealing more intricacies of the web of life. They show embedded human beings are in complex ecosystems and how deeply dependent they are on other life forms. As human beings, we are not merely part of humankind; rather we should see ourselves as "*Earthlings*" – as members of a very diverse Earth community or even "Citizens of the Cosmos." This shift in perspective invites us to contemplate humanity's own evolutionary process. It necessitates us to rethink our role as humans within a broader eco-context. We believe it means the de-centering of the *Anthropos*, and re-centering of human life within and not separate from other species and organisms with whom we share the planet.

This new perspective is very clearly expressed in the *Earth Charter*, a document of the United Nations that has been added as a supplement to the Universal Declaration of Human Rights. The Earth Charter states:

> Humanity is part of a vast evolving universe. Earth, our home, is alive with a unique community of life. The forces of nature make existence a demanding and uncertain adventure, but Earth has provided the conditions essential to life's evolution. The resilience of the community of life and the well-being of humanity depend upon preserving a healthy biosphere with all its ecological systems, a rich variety of plants and animals, fertile soils, pure waters, and clean air. The global environment with its finite resources is a common concern of all peoples. The protection of Earth's vitality, diversity, and beauty is a sacred trust.[12]

Nature," and "Beyond the Enlightenment Mentality," both in Mary Evelyn Tucker and John Berthrong, eds, *Confucianism and Ecology* (Cambridge, MA: Harvard University Press, 1998).

12.   See http://www.earthcharterinaction.org/content/pages/Read-the-Charter.html.

This new interpretation of the Human-Earth relationship calls for enormous creativity. It activates not only a desire for new knowledge, values and understanding of who we are as human beings, but also activates new sensitivities and imagination and seriously challenges our current humanist conception of human agency, autonomy and responsibility. This new interpretation requires humanists to develop a new ethic that takes into consideration new evolutionary insights that do not just consider human beings, but all interdependent life forms. It means all life forms serve as the primary and founding value of humanism.

The development of this new ethic could draw on studies demonstrating how various cultures have maintained a rich and more open appreciation of the nonhuman world than imagined within humanism and its paradigm of modernity.[13] Such knowledge can be used to question the principal value distinction between humans and nonhumans underpinning a modern ethical paradigm. In this way, attention to culture not framed by this centering of humans provides a method for fostering greater focus on complex structures of continuities and discontinuities between different life forms. We believe humanism can reinvent new principles of solidarity, dignity and interaction between different life forms.

Everyday Humanism: Knowledge, Passion and Action

Earlier we argued the global ecological crisis is fundamentally a crisis of values. A critical reflection on religious and non-religious worldviews and their value frames may be helpful if we hope to understand the emergence of the current ecological crisis.

Our brief exploration of the history of humanism outlines the manner in which humanism brought much good in the world in terms of human dignity (at least for certain groups) and democratic values, but neglected humanity's relationship with nature and the interdependence of all living organisms on Earth. In this way humanist values have played a role in the emergence of the ecological crisis. We, therefore, argue in favor of a shift from a *human*-centered to a *life*-centered humanist worldview. We believe that humanist sources of knowledge and values can be positively applied in this process of transformation. We conclude by offering some suggestions on how to start a turnaround by focusing on three dimensions of change: (a) Knowledge, (b) Passion and (c) Action.

13.   See, for instance, Philippe Descola, *Par-delà nature et culture* (Paris: Gallimard, 2005).

Knowledge

Humanism has long been characterized by its open and appreciative attitude
to science and rationality. Humanism has consistently encouraged innova-
tion through the application of new scientific insights. However, this "natural kinship" between humanism and science has now entered a new phase.
During the last century, our scientific knowledge about the evolution, life
and human beings has increased rapidly. New insights, which emerged from
diverse scientific domains, ranging from space and Earth sciences to micro-
biology, have gradually produced a new integrated picture of the evolution
of life on Earth. This picture shows strong symbiotic relationships between
diverse life forms. The dynamics of interdependence are much more profound and complex than previously assumed. These contemporary scientific
discoveries ought to instil a sense of modesty and wonder in us. The more
we know, the more there is we do not yet know. The vastness of the cosmos
with its countless mysterious dimensions might fill us with feelings of awe
and wonderment. Humanists may want to take note of these developments.
The French philosopher Edgar Morin expresses it like this: "The life the
Earth has produced which it enjoys, which we enjoy, is possibly unique in
the cosmos. It does not flow from any a-priori necessity. It is probably alone
in the solar system, fragile, rare, and precious because rare and fragile."[14]

New available scientific knowledge and perceptions of modesty and
enthusiasm challenge humanism in the twenty-first century to open itself
up to new fundamental questions about life on Earth and the role of human
beings in that process of life. We pointed to some of these questions earlier in this chapter, questions such as: how can we connect the idea of a
broader community of life and the fundamental interdependency between
humans and other life forms with existing essentialist humanist values of
autonomy and freedom? How can we give new substance to critical humanist notions of human development and human flourishing? And perhaps
the most important question of all: does the intensive growth of scientific
and technological developments of the last decennia re-situate the human
being within the broader community of life in radically new ways? As Paul
Hawken reminded us: human beings now have the capacity to actively "alter
the fate of all living beings" due to our impact on the Earth.

If it is true that humanity is capable of altering the evolution of life on
Earth, then what kind of new responsibilities does that entail? Or to put it
differently: should human beings in the twenty-first century play a proactive

14.   Edgar Morin and Anne Brigitte Kern, *Homeland Earth: A Manifesto for the
New Millennium* (New York: Hampton Press, 1999), p. 45.

role in the preservation and further development of life on Earth? We believe that humanists can draw on their rich sources and traditions to address these important questions.

Passion

Humanism is much more than science and reason. It has a rich historical tradition in the world of arts and culture. In addition to an intellectual and scientific shift, we propose human beings need to actively cultivate a passionate aesthetic sense of human-Earth relationships to which they can relate affectively. Creative expressions of people's deep intuitions and experiences of the more-than-human world can help to engage people in new ways of experiencing the world. Carol Wintermute also encourages humanists to more deeply explore the "aesthetic pillar of Humanism"[15] and integrate the mind and emotions in an aesthetic dimension of life. Here she refers to John Dewey who broadened the humanist horizon by arguing that truth can be found in the artistic experience as well as in science and reason. Furthermore, in *Political Emotions: Why Love Matters for Justice*, Martha Nussbaum questions the political tendency to focus on respect as the only critical public emotion necessary for a "good" society.[16] Nussbaum argues that respect alone is insufficient, because it is cold and too inactive to overcome what she sees as humanity's tendency towards exploitation. Nor is respect grounded in human dignity sufficient to overcome inequality. Love, says Nussbaum, is at the heart of all of the essential emotions that sustain a decent society. She defines love as the "intense attachment to things outside the control of our will" and argues that public emotions have two important sides, namely an institutional and a motivational. In terms of the latter, love, says Nussbaum, can play a valuable role in transforming distant and abstract principles into a more personal "circle of concern." Cultivating love for the Earth and expressing this love in a commitment to change could play an important role in bringing the human-Earth relationship into humanity's "circle of concern." The humanist love for values of equality, rule of law and democracy could deepen our commitment to living within the ecological limitations of the Earth.

15.   Carol Wintermute, "The Aesthetic Pillar of Humanism," *Humanism Today* 13 (1999), published by the North American Committee for Humanism (NACH). See www.humanismtoday.org/vol13/wintermute.html
16.   Martha C. Nussbaum, *Political Emotions: Why Love matters for Justice* (Cambridge, MA: The Belknap Press of Harvard University, 2013), p. 11.

Action

"Green" has steadily become an attractive quality in the realm of action over the last years. An ever-growing number of people seem to be driven by a desire to engage in concrete action for green change. They focus on issues such as sustainable food production and renewable energy; they invent ecologically sustainable lifestyle projects or promote the protection of nature's biodiversity. By mapping a plethora of such activities in *Blessed Unrest*, Paul Hawken draws attention to worldwide green initiatives and new seemingly unstoppable green dynamics.[17] A new way of life seems to manifest. Some even speak of The *Great Transformation*[18] or of a "million quiet revolutions."[19] But, even more than through ideas and stories, people seem to be energized by actively participating in concrete, small and large initiatives for sustainable change. Their response to many of the rather sombre predictions about life on Earth is one of action, of actually doing. This capacity to act can generate new optimism and hope. Out of all living beings on Earth, evolution shows human beings are capable of radical adaptation and change, particularly when in serious trouble. In *The Great Disruption*[20] Paul Gilding suggests this quality is what distinguishes human beings from other living beings. A second dimension of this "green wave" of action is the fact that it involves actions that are only loosely connected. Rather than being formally managed through institutions, they often are initiated through a "bottom up" approach and fuelled by radical democratic inspiration. New information technologies and social media, which are accessible and affordable to people everywhere, offer important sources of inspiration and the possibilities to share experiences. The form these "green actions" may take can dissipate and "then re-gather quickly, without central leadership, command or control. Rather than seeking dominance, this unnamed movement strives to disperse concentrations of power."[21] Such ways of being "active" resonate with values such as creativity, enthusiasm, and freedom – all deeply rooted

17. Hawken, *Blessed Unrest*.
18. Paul Raskin *et al.*, *Great Transition: The Promise and the Lure of the Times Ahead* (Stockholm: Stockholm Environmental Institute, 2002).
19. Bénédicte Manier, *Un million de eévolutions tranquilles. Travail/ argent/ habitat/ santé/ environment. Comment les citoyens changent le monde.* (Paris: les Liens qui libèrent, 2012).
20. Paul Gilding, *The Great Disruption: How the Climate Crisis Will Transform the Global Economy* (London: Bloomsbury Press, 2011).
21. Hawken, *Blessed Unrest*. Throughout this book, Hawken reminds us that human beings now have the capacity to actively alter the fate of all living beings due to their impact on the Earth.

in humanist traditions. The green "movement" thus offers a great opportunity for humanism to re-invigorate its own insights and inspirations in this regard. The ability for change through action may provide a solid basis from which to reconceptualize humanism as an inspiration for sustainable life on Earth.

10 On the Limits of Charity

Anthony B. Pinn[*]

The opportunities are overwhelming, countless really. The need is great, and it's global in reach and tenacious in its intensity. Television, radio, magazines – these and other information outlets offer occasions for engaging in this, for offering one's resources to those with a less robust set of resources. The need is all around and it presents itself in so many ways.

What I have in mind is the various ways during the course of the typical day we are invited to give – to be charitable. Whether it's the homeless person's request for assistance, disasters of various types, destruction of the environment and so on, in uncomfortable ways, this is the stuff of human existence, the dark corners of life. And so, the question for humanists, as I understand it, doesn't involve simple denouncing of the theologically derived modes of giving embraced by theists – although they warrant critique. A more creative step is also necessary and that involves how and what humanists should think about giving, about charity, not simply as a reactive stance against theism but as a fundamental dimension of humanism in practice.

The Nature of Charity

I think there is something about Steven Pinker's understanding of the psychology of human interaction that is applicable here – something about his

[*]   Anthony B. Pinn is the Agnes Cullen Arnold Professor of Humanities and Professor of Religious Studies at Rice University. Pinn is founding director of Rice's Center for Engaged Research and Collaborative Learning. He is also the Director of Research for the Institute for Humanist Studies. He is the author/editor of 30 books including, *African American Humanist Principles* (2004); *By These Hands: A Documentary History of African American Humanism* (2001); *The End of God-Talk* (2012) and *Writing God's Obituary: How a Good Methodist Became a Better Atheist* (2014). In 1999 he received the African American Humanist Award from the Council for Secular Humanism, and in 2006 he was named Harvard Humanist of the Year.

understanding of when and why people are altruistic that lends itself to issues of charity of concern to us in this chapter. As scholars have noted, human societies are marked by the infrastructures, arrangements, and models of living that involve tools for inequality, pain, suffering, and a general messiness. Humans are primed for competition and its consequences.[1] While this is part of natural selection, there is something about us that also allows for at least a momentary bracketing of such drives marked by giving, by charity, by aiding those who on some level – in a world of limited resource and a thrust for survival – are the competition.

In a way, charity is a part of natural selection – the effort to keep members of the human species moving along. This is because in certain circumstances charitable moves are about survival and continuation. It isn't always nice, and isn't a matter of warm regard. It can be more strategic than that. In a word, acts of charity or compassion benefit in some way the one doing the good. Put differently, giving away things of value speaks to the status and the achievements of the giver in that he or she is able to do without whatever it is he or she has bestowed on the other.[2] In a sense, generosity or charity can be read as saying "I am better than you; I have more than you, and in recognition of my superior status…here, take this." This is not to say the receiver of the gift makes no gain or secures no advantage as a result, the person or organization certainly does. But it is an advantage given by one who still has the upper hand.[3]

There is something harsh sounding about this reality, and it can be difficult to stomach as a moral principle. We, however, have developed communicative devises and skills to address this. Doctrines and creeds, as well as methods of display (for example, rituals and ethics) constitute one such communicative device, complete with formal structures of thought. The more biological and psychological dimensions of this taking and giving are coded through a spiritualization of the process, a linking of it to greater forces at work in the world. Religious creeds and theological formulations of the human point to this, although there is an effort to soften this position through appeals to cosmic moral measures as the ultimate source for and sustainer of generosity and charity. After all, within Christianity for instance, the god figure gives the ultimate gift to undeserving and rebellious humans: God surrenders a portion of God's self in order to redeem

1.   Steven Pinker, *How the Mind Works* (New York: W. W. Norton, 1999, 2009), p. 427.
2.   Pinker, *How the Mind Works*, pp. 499–500.
3.   Pinker, *How the Mind Works*, p. 502.

fallen humanity.[4] What Christianity and other theisms attempt to do is push generosity beyond family and others within the circle of intimacy to a more general population. Theists have well documented strategies and rationales for giving, but are such strategies only possible if there is a god or gods in place? Don't humanist also have (or at least need to develop) ways to publicly articulate the basis for and meaning of charity – whether as a biological and/or psychological development or something else deeply human?

The answer is clearly "yes," or why else this chapter?

A significant percentage of US citizens participate in charitable giving in some way, shape, or form. In this way, one might argue "giving," is deeply connected to the structures of living in the United States – this despite the clear signs of bias, oppression, and inequality that mark urban and rural landscapes of these states. The numerous infomercials and special programs meant to document need and request funds speak to at least a tested assumption that US citizens have money and/or time to give and are willing to give it at least in modest ways. While charity is a big deal, it has met with mixed reviews.

Some argue charity is superficial attention to deep issues. That is to say, it doesn't actually solve problems because it doesn't alter systems, in that it doesn't provide skills that allow people to sustain themselves. Instead, as Robert Lupton argues, charity creates dependency. "Giving to those in need what they could be gaining from their own initiative," he argues, "may well be the kindest way to destroy people." It reduces individual accountability and simply re-enforces the problem that giving to others – for example, charity – is meant to alleviate.[5] Something of this position gives the impression, at least to me, of pathology, or of capacity. That is to say, it seems to assume getting the disadvantaged *to do*, without adequate attention to the systemic circumstance that create and perpetuate their predicament (e.g., racism, sexism, homophobia, classism) solves the problem of inequality and need. *Really?* Do the poor actually remain poor because they aren't encouraged to make a difference in their own lives? Isn't this similar to claiming the inequality felt by many African Americans isn't systemic but rather it is a moral failure on the part of African Americans? For instance, this argument – charity is harmful to self-motivation – might suggest African Americans (or substitute another group) would appeal less for assistance *if* they were better conditioned and encouraged to do the right thing on their own. *Really, it's that simple?*

According to figures like Lupton, when charity is given under such circumstances it has more to do with the giver of the gift than the person(s)

---

4.   Pinker, *How the Mind Works*, pp. 428–29.
5.   Robert D. Lupton, *Toxic Charity: How Churches and Charities Hurt Those They Help (and How to Reverse It)* (New York: HarperOne, 2011), pp. 4–5.

receiving, in that the former is giving the latter something he/she should secure on their own. Lupton would have us believe this is the case because charity is premised on the emotional and psychological benefit to the giver as opposed to the wellbeing of those receiving the assistance. In a word, charity fosters the very attitudes and approaches it seeks to redress. In the short term it might appear beneficial, but this giving has limited long-term utility.[6] Yet, there is an element to this equation often ignored: much of the fundamental economic inequality that breeds the call for charity has something to do with the ongoing ramifications of slavery and colonialism through means of which certain populations were dehumanized and were used as a source of labor. These populations in the "global South" continue to struggle to surmount systemic modes of discrimination. Address the legacy of enslavement and colonialism – perhaps through reparations – and we will have gone a long way in addressing the very need for charity in a variety of locations.

Charity and Theism

Is a different attitude toward charity, toward giving to those in need, possible if charity is framed in terms of theism? Within that context, charity is almost surely viewed through a theological lens that visualizes it as obligation fulfilled as a sign of one's righteousness, closeness to cosmic realities, and growth as a spiritual individual. The point of giving under such circumstances always privileges the giver's relationship to the ultimate giver – the cosmic "something(s)" – with the receiver being a conduit. In this way, it is a reflexive recognition of humanity – the personhood of the disadvantaged is affirmed only in light of how we might feel in similar circumstances.

According to some, religious persons tend to be happier and in certain ways healthier than the general population.[7] A cosmic blindfold that protects against viewing the more tragic and ambiguous dimensions of human experience might account for this happiness. A link between this general affirming stance toward the world and good done by theists through the expressions of this happiness – charitable giving and service – is assumed.[8] Yet, it's chemical in essence: religion produces a state of mind that connects the self to "something," promotes empathy and encourages the body to

6.   Lupton, *Toxic Charity*, pp. 4–6.
7.   Paul J. Zak, *The Moral Molecule: The Source of Love and Prosperity* (New York: Dutton, 2012), pp. 132–33.
8.   Zak, *Moral Molecule*, pp. 132–33.

release oxytocin, which is associated with moral behavior. That is, "unless the release of oxytocin is impaired, the Golden Rule is a lesson the body already knows, and when we get it right we feel the rewards immediately."[9] We feel the rewards: is giving really about the giver? Yet, this "moral molecule," as Paul Zak calls it, doesn't rule out the possibility of selfishness, of self-centered motivations.[10]

There aren't simply biological – chemical – considerations at play with issues such as charity or giving in a more general sense. As Steven Pinker has aptly noted, humans do a variety of things that relate to the maintenance of human life, but there are a variety of activities such as religion that make no substantive contribution to these basic drives. These are addressed, hence, not through biological considerations primarily but through psychology.[11]

As Christians are wont to say, following the phrase often attributed to the martyr John Bradford, "There but for the grace of God go I." This statement, intended to reflect a certain mindfulness and piety, highlights the workings of mysterious grace in the world – but undergirding this is a feeling of difference, a sense that something has been done that distinguishes the viewer and the person or situation being viewed. Missing from this is the ability to view the humanity of the other simply based on the assumed – not reflected – humanity of the other.

Humanity restricted to reflected humanity ("you are like me") is a dilemma, and I don't see a way out of this dilemma for theists.

It is embedded in their theological-ethical understanding of the human and the path to proper fellowship with the divine; it is grounded in a basic missionary impulse that fuels so much religious activity, particularly on the part of evangelical Christian churches in the United States. In a very significant way, this approach to human need is part of Christian theism's DNA. In short, for theists, such as Christians, compassion is a less significant concern regarding generosity while it is a significant factor for humanists. Put differently, humanists may be motivated to exercise generosity, or in this case charity, as a consequence of emotional connection to others grounded in empathy with the predicament of others. And this is over against theists, who "may ground their generosity less in emotion and more in other factors such as doctrine, a communal identity, or reputational concerns."[12] Theists

9.   Zak, *Moral Molecule*, p. xviii.
10.   Zak, *Moral Molecule*, pp. 146–47, xii–xiii.
11.   Pinker, *How the Mind Works*, p. 521.
12.   Laura R. Saslow *et al.*, "My Brother's Keeper? Compassion Predicts Generosity More among Less Religious Individuals," *Social Psychological and Personality Science* (April 26, 2012), p.7: http://spp.sagepub.com/content/early/2012/04/25/1948550612444137.

may provide assistance and use theological concepts such as God to arrange this behavior, but this process of placement doesn't speak necessarily to a deep regard for others or for greater compassion. Rather, it points toward the other as a means to an end: through service the giver confirms or asserts his or her self in relationship to a divine or cosmic force ordaining the activity. In essence, charity or the good is performed *for* this cosmic agent, *to* the unfortunate.[13] The argument has been over who gives (and gives more) and why give. Addressing this has consumed a good deal of energy on the part of humanist and atheists.

Charity and Humanists

I don't agree with Lupton, but his remarks provide an interesting opening to explore theistic structuring of charity and to then frame alternate humanist approaches.

Again, there are ways in which this compassion in theists is mitigated through a larger connection to perceived cosmic forces, so that the primary concern in giving to others isn't simply compassion for them in and of itself but rather the manner in which the act of giving links the giver to a spiritual command and to a cosmic force, often called God or gods. Whereas studies suggest that for nontheists compassion in and of itself is a prime motivation for giving. Yet, even secular ideals can provide a function similar to God – motivating involvement and generosity as a right act.[14]

Not content to give, nontheists, and rightfully so, are committed to making certain it is known publicly that they give not in spite of their humanism but as a direct result of their humanist ethics and moral outlook – as the religious claim their spiritual commitments, doctrines and creeds inform (if not demand) their contributions to the wellbeing of those who are suffering.[15] There are ways in which humanist organizations work to maximize the impact of giving by: (1) promoting giving with a limited percentage of donations going into administration and so on, and (2) promoting giving to charitable organizations that are in line with humanist values and goals. Put another way, "the greater good of humanity is promoted when we help others to the

13.   Azim F. Shariff and Ara Norenzayan, "God is Watching You: Priming God Concepts Increases Prosocial Behavior in an Anonymous Economic Game," *Psychological Science* 18.9 (2007), pp. 803–809, esp. 803.

14.   Saslow *et al.*, "My Brother's Keeper?"; Shariff and Norenzayan, "God is Watching You," p. 806.

15.   Jessica Williams, "Faith, Hope and Charity," *New Humanist* (May 31, 2007). http://rationalist.org.uk/articles/941/faith-hope-and-charity.

best of our abilities. Not everyone can donate every time, nor can everyone give the large amounts all charities look for – we all know that the economic realities of these times make that difficult. But as humanists we do care for others in circumstances detached from our locale and immediate family."[16] An underlying, but perhaps unintended, consequence of humanist apologetics for charitable giving is a rather unproductive debate over who gives and why, with little impact on the systemic arrangements of life that under gird the need. It's a "me too" attitude toward need that secretly puts the focus of attention on the giver rather than the underlying structures of societal living that undergird the "lack" which charity superficially addresses. I say superficially because such giving typically leaves unchallenged structural inequality based on things such as racial discrimination, gender-bias, class stratification, and so on.

One might think nontheists' interest in charity is one example of them moving beyond monitoring theism's presence in the public (and private), a shift of attention and focus away from what theists are doing, and more concern with sharing the best of nontheistic orientation with the world through care for the pain of the world. But the typical, public perception of nontheistic orientations in the United States, the continuing bias against those without firm theistic religious inclinations, makes it more than difficult for humanists and other nontheists to direct their energy in any particular direction without some consideration of how theists will understand the effort and what it might mean with respect to the perception of humanists. Public relations is always and already a dimension of the humanist vision and effort because the "fit" of nontheists in the socio-cultural fabric of life in the United States and elsewhere is perpetually open to questioning.[17]

Whether resting content in critique of the god-motivation for generosity and charity on the part of theists, humanists might give greater consideration to the dilemma embedded in godless giving. That is to say, like theists, there are ways in which nontheistic charity prioritizes adherence to principles and the mirror-effect (for example, the other in need is like me). In both cases, charity is premised on the giver and this makes it much more difficult to target underlying issues. In both instances, reputation of the giver is a factor. Approaches to giving that are not premised on those in need makes it too easy to avoid the underlying and systemic challenges that promote

16.   "An Open Letter to Humanists: Donating to Humanist Charities." http://americanhumanist.org/HNN/details/2011-09-an-open-letter-to-humanists-donating-to-humanist-cha.

17.   Richard Cimino and Christopher Smith, "The New Atheism and the Formation of the Imagined Secularist Community," *Journal of Media and Religion* 10.1 (2011), pp. 24–38, esp. 25–26.

and reproduce inequality and need. For example, while "Humanist Team on Kiva" offers loans to small companies as a way to generate economic growth, what of the underlying modalities of injustice and discrimination that produce the inequality such loans seek to address?[18]

Charity begets more charity, not because those receiving it have some sort of moral failure or lack necessary capacities and motivation; but because charity doesn't address the underlying structures of inequality that support the infrastructures of harm. Poor housing easily destroyed by powerful storms, the geographic placement of poverty that makes the poor targets for what we have come to call "environmental racism," the political corruption and limited training that makes medical care difficult to secure and maintain, are just some of the internal social structures that feed our collective demise. Those not as hampered by these structures, not as sensitive to shifts in the flow of power – for example, social positions, political policies, and so on – give bits of what is available. This is not to belittle charity, nor to question the need to give, but rather what I offer here is meant to contextual this giving, to provide a genealogy of sorts for the problems motivating compassion.

In an odd way, the typical mode of charity is disembodied in that it separates the giver from that which receives the charity. That is to say, focus on charity as opposed to the substrata – the situation that demands attention: the cause rather than simply the cost – is a problem. Those suffering – whether human animals, other animals, the natural environment and so on – become an abstraction, an idea, to which we respond in ways that require no real engagement with the suffering experienced and its root causes. It is this level of conversation, the embodied nature of structures of living, that humanism should be well positioned to understand and tackle.

We, on some level, give in order to safeguard the public perception of the godless – to not come across as godless life is a selfish and anti-communal existence. *And, we should continue to give, but not as an "end," but as a fill-gap as we work to recognize and trouble the infrastructure of inequality that feed ongoing and complex needs.* It is related to these larger systemic issues where charity and public policy might be held in tension. That is to say, charity – giving of resources – has to be tied to re-envisioning the terms and language of collective life. Do the little things matter, the contributions to charities sparked by the narrative of a particular tragedy? Of course, but as a bandage that might tell us more about those giving than the social arrangements that prescribe such situations.

18.   British Humanist Association, "Good Causes and Charities," https://humanism.org.uk/humanism/humanism-today/humanists-doing/good-causes-and-charities/.

Humanists should be aware of this, and should recognize that dollars given must be tied to policies and collective practices of life that short-circuit the causes of our traumas.

There might also be a need for a different attitude on the part of humanists involved in charity. Recognition of structural barriers might make necessary a different sense of ethic's impact on living conditions. Put differently, many theists give in connection with their efforts to model their deities and with a sense that cosmic forces are involved in the struggle against pain and misery, providing a mode of consistent presence and impact humans alone can't achieve. Nontheists, however, are guided by a different perception of transformation. Without cosmic assistance of any type, the likelihood of sustained change that eventually wipes out the need for charity and structural change is questionable at best. That is to say, giving and policy activism are not undertaken because they guarantee anything but rather because they are what *we can do*.

Sisyphus is the model here: the struggle is perpetual, but without producing nihilism. What I propose is tied to Albert Camus's sense of ethics. Charity is often self-serving and of no long-term consequence and long-term transformation is unlikely. This is a recasting of charity, lessening its "feel good" quality and highlighting the tangled nature of our systemic challenges. It is to imagine ourselves happy as we struggle in a world in our relationship with which we encounter the absurd.[19] This ethical and moral posture avoids some of the hyper-optimism of earlier forms of humanism and sees through the human to connections and intersections of life.

Charity so conceived becomes a marker of relationship – a symbol of relationship – but without substantial consequence.

Giving of Oneself

Perhaps charity is the wrong term for what we are to do with our resources, perhaps it is a misnaming of what we are engaged in? Transformation is too grand a claim for what our efforts can produce. We work in the short term and long term because it is what we can do within our situation and in light of our circumstances: Nothing more, and nothing less. Utopias aren't possible, and many of the ways in which charity is perceived – particularly its assumed

19.   Read this in light of Albert Camus' *The Myth of Sisyphus and Other Essays* (New York: Vintage International, 1991). In particular I have in mind the title essay for that volume. I also write in response to Camus' *The Rebel* (New York: Vintage International, 1991).

potential – tend to imply the possibility of altered space in which life has full integrity and robustness. I suggest such thinking doesn't fit humanism well and runs contrary to what we know of human action and inclinations.

Some would argue what I propose is without hope; hence, it is a position entailing nihilism. Even the insightful atheist and philosopher A. C. Grayling makes such a claim concerning the loss of hope. "It is taken for a truism that hope is essential to life," Grayling writes. He continues, "what would it be to have no hopes, to believe that things only get worse, to expect failure and anticipate defeat? That is scarcely conceivable."[20] Yet, as theologian and philosopher Juergen Manemann has reminded me on more than one occasion, hope is impossible without despair. Those who have not encountered despair have no grounds for hope.[21] Oddly enough my position is closer to that held by Manemann, minus his sense in which the divine figures into the maintenance of hope. I argue for a hope against hope. That is to say, I suggest a position, or posture toward the world, in which our affirmations, or in this case our claims to giving as having sustainable impact, must be negated by recognition of our deep failures and the structural challenges to noteworthy change. Hence, we act simply because we can, despite the inherent limitations in doing so.

We hope against our hope; we labor despite our failings. This is to live, as Henry David Thoreau would appreciate, knowing that we have lived. And this is a living that is humble to some degree, aware, generous but always noting the haunting limitations of even our best efforts.

I think humanists are often too optimistic, a trait shared with theists but with a different grounding. We assume our efforts, if sincere, will produce results; we've brought this line of thinking forward from the Enlightenment. But is it really justified? And if it is not, as I believe it isn't, what does it mean to give? What does it mean to surrender some of one's own holdings – in whatever form – to benefit others?

Our giving might be considered a celebration of life. It is recognition of connection and relationship that includes life beyond the confines of our individual selves.

The importance of charity in this way isn't the actual giving as if it alters the large and imposing systems of our collective lives, but rather it is a

---

20.   A. C. Grayling, "Hope," in *Meditations for the Humanist: Ethics for a Secular Age* (Oxford: Oxford University Press, 2002), p. 34. Interestingly enough, Grayling does not provide explicit commentary on the notion of "charity." He comes closest in the chapter on "gifts."

21.   Said during a conversation on November 4, 2013, at the Hannover Institute for Philosophical Research, Hannover, Germany. This is a general principle of his version of German Political Theology and moral philosophy.

statement of regard for the web of life of which we are a part. It is a glance in the direction of the "other" in various forms. Charity, hence, entails fragile recognition of our connectedness and mindfulness that weighs our individual existence over against another dimension of the natural world and reaches to share something of our holdings.[22] While disagreeing with his theistic orientation, perhaps there is something that speaks to the intent of charity in the words of theologian and minister Howard Thurman, who says, "to be alive is to participate responsibly in the experience of life."[23]

There is something of relevance here in Thoreau's urging readers of Walden to embrace a deliberate life, one through which we know, at the end, we have lived. This is more than the typical and rather easy efforts that capture what we mean by charity, giving, or a humanitarian posture toward the world. Such effort and its framing is, for him, too easy. "A man," he writes, "is not a good man to me because he will feed me if I should be starving, or warm me if I should be freezing, or pull me out of a ditch if I should ever fall into one. I can find a Newfoundland Dog that will do as much." A dog that can give this type of basic assistance because such action does not push us to address root causes of injustice and misery, does not force us to fix ourselves to the extent we participate in injustice and does not demand attention to the restructuring of the organizational framing of life that confines us to less than ideal ways of being to ourselves and with the world. In a word, turning again to Thoreau, "there are a thousand hacking at the branches of evil to one who is striking at the root, and it may be that he who bestows the largest amount of time and money on the needy is doing the most by his mode of life to produce that misery which he strives in vain to relive." Charity - giving - as a mode of living with others is something that Thoreau critiques and theism typically embraces. I side with Thoreau in that charity demands little of us and does not expose much of us to others. In this way, it may take thought and may be categorized as a "sacrifice" but it is rather easy and of limited depth. It is what Thoreau would label "doing good," when we should strive to "be good," and let the rest follow from that. (But, I would note, this is not Lupton's "up by their own bootstraps," in that it recognizes systemic issues, for Thoreau slavery, and for us a host of related concerns.) Thoreau encourages us to give deeply of ourselves, to recognize the value of life, and to act in ways that speak to this depth – to move beyond what is easy (or that which is of our first mind) and

22.   Many of these ideas are more fully developed in Anthony B. Pinn, *The End of God-Talk: An African American Humanist Theology* (New York: Oxford University Press, 2012).

23.   Pinn, *End of God-Talk*, p. 128.

to *be* what we seek to achieve for others. In an important sense, I would suggest, Thoreau offers a sense of giving that means being vulnerable, exposed, involved, yet fully aware that poor situations will likely persist despite our efforts to buttress the integrity of individual and collective life.[24]

And we might call this our practices of shared existence. This, in the end, may only amount to a small improvement in the ability to have a good death. Or, as Alice Walker reflects, "it must become a right of every person to die of old age. And if we secure this right for ourselves, we can, coincidentally, assure it for the planet. And that, as they say, will be excellent, which is, perhaps, only another name for health."[25] Perhaps rather than talk of charity and charitable acts as the basic parameters of our ethics in action, humanists should present themselves as concerned and engaged in ways that recognize the fragility of human concern, the persistence of structures of injustice (in which we participate)? Yet, all this might be modified by our acknowledgement that we push against barriers to healthy existence for all life because it is what we can try to do; it is our last best option. Rather than calling this charity, we might simply say it is to live, and to live in ways that allow life.

24.   Quotations are from Henry David Thoreau, *Walden* (Princeton: Princeton University Press, 1973), pp. 74–76. Found in Pinn, *End of God-Talk*. The general ideas found related to ethics here as they revolve around Thoreau and Thurman are from *End of God-Talk*.

25.   Alice Walker, "Longing to Die of Old Age," in Walker, *Living by the Word* (New York: Harcourt Bracer Jovanovich, 1988), p. 36.

11 On Thinking about an Advance Care Directive

Katrina Scott[*]

Prologue

I met Mrs D one afternoon walking down the hall, guiding not pushing her IV pole. Her sturdy white sneakers were a give-away to her outlook on life. No soft-grip socks for her. We walked and talked about her upcoming surgery to replace a heart valve. Upbeat and cheery, she looked forward to taking mile-long walks again without feeling faint. We spoke about family and life at home, the upcoming election, and her positive attitude on almost everything. For example, she was the lucky one; she had bed B, next to the big glass window with a fabulous view of the Charles River. Over the next week we walked and talked often; I met her husband and one of her daughters. She confided her husband was against the surgery, and although he was angry, she wanted to go for it because life was not worth living halfway. After all, at 91, what did she have to lose? She had lived a good life; death would not be a tragedy. In order to proceed, she was "full code," meaning everything would be done to keep her alive during surgery.

I visited Mrs D in the cardiac ICU. The heart surgery was a success, but she suffered neurological damage that left her essentially in a persistent vegetative state (PVS) but not brain-dead. Intubated and receiving hydration, the

[*] Katrina Scott received her Masters of Divinity from Harvard Divinity School and is the Oncology Chaplain at Massachusetts General Hospital, where she provides spiritual support to patients, family and staff. She is the author of several articles on the National Consensus Project for Quality Palliative Care (NCP) *Clinical Practice Guidelines Domain 5*: "Spiritual, Religious and Existential Aspects for Care" (2008) and is dedicated to promoting a multi-disciplinary team approach to end-of-life care. Endorsed by the American Ethical Union (Ethical Culture) for Health Care Chaplaincy, Katrina is an Officiant of the Ethical Society of Boston and Board Certified by the Association of Professional Chaplains.

ICU staff slowly began to lessen her sedation. There was no response; her husband of 66 years would arrive every morning and park his walker all day by her side, wishing "she'd wake up." Teary-eyed, Mr D often said, "Just tell me what to do." I told him about our past conversations; how she had never envisioned anything other than a return to a good life or a quick death.

Days became weeks. During a family meeting with her attending (the "successful" cardiologist: the neurologist was not present), the family did not want to give up on the possibility that she might awake some day. "She did everything for us…we can't let her down now." It was decided to follow a three-to-six-month time line to "see how she's doing." Mrs D was moved to an acute care hospital closer to her home in western Massachusetts. I am unsure if she is still there.

Introduction

"One in five Americans die using ICU services. The doubling of persons over the age of 65 yrs by 2030 will require a system-wide expansion in ICU care for dying patients unless the healthcare system pursues rationing, more effective advance care planning, and augmented capacity to care for dying patients in other settings."[1] Dr Mitchell Levy's editorial response to this sobering data was revealing: "In a manner of speaking, we could say that death is now the most common illness in the ICU."[2] Approximately half of all patients who die in the hospital are cared for in an ICU within three days of their death. Given the large number of people who die this way, (540,000 or 20 percent of all Americans), how our health care system handles these daily events was rapidly recognized as a significant public health concern.[3]

1. Dr Derek Angus *et al.*, "Use of Intensive Care at the End of Life in the United States: An Epidemiologic Study," *Critical Care Medicine* 32 (2004), pp. 638–43. This study (supported by the Robert Wood Johnson Foundation and an NIA grant) incorporated all non-federal hospital discharge data from 1999 from six states and the National Death Index for analysis. This was the first study to calculate the number of Americans who receive ICU care at end of life.

2. Dr Levy teaches at Brown University School of Medicine. His editorial "Dying in America," *Critical Care Medicine* 32.3 (March 2004), was one of many responses appearing in numerous journals to Angus *et al.*

3. ICU stays have not changed, but the number of hospital deaths of EOL patients decreased from 2007–2010, from 28.1 percent to 25 percent of all deaths. David C. Goodman *et al.*, "Tracking Improvement in the Care of Chronically Ill Patients: Dartmouth Atlas Brief," *Dartmouth Institute for Health Policy*

Along with the physical and financial problems of sheer volume and cost, there are numerous complex medical, ethical and psychosocial issues surrounding death in the ICU.

Still considered the acme of technological intervention in medicine, the goal of restoring health through successful treatment and acute care has slowly changed over the last decade as more patients with non-reversible medical conditions are admitted into these units for life-sustaining treatment. This trend of aggressively treating patients suffering from incurable advanced disease as well as irreversible surgical trauma often stems from an uninformed decision for which patients and families bear the ultimate consequences. Think of the many TV dramas that show a person's total recovery from a severe injury requiring CPR (cardiopulmonary resuscitation) in which they literally walk away.[4] In fact, in many cases the ICU is now used as a death-management tool; in buying extra time for family and loved ones to gather at the dying person's bedside, to assuage our feeling that "we did all we could," and in rare cases, to cover fears of malpractice claims for hastened death.

Although how physicians approach decision-making when caring for critically ill patients is inadequately understood, the acknowledged reluctance of physicians to predict death, along with the complementary link between prognosis and therapy, adversely effect decision-making in patient care.[5] Simply put, when given the ability to offer treatment even in "medically futile" cases, the majority of physicians will opt for end-stage therapy over comfort-only measures.[6] Results of the five-year, 30 million dollar *Study to Understand Prognoses and Preferences for Outcomes and Risks of*

and Clinical Practice. June 2013. Others disagree with this study's methodology/findings, including palliative care physician Diane Meier.

4.   Television misleads you by letting you think a person will be healthy enough to go home about 67 percent of the time. Susan J. Diem *et al,*. "Cardiopulmonary Resuscitation on Television — Miracles and Misinformation," *New England Journal of Medicine* 334.24 (1996), pp. 1578–82. In reality, if CPR is able to bring the patient back to life, the chance of this person going home with good brain function is about 7 percent. For other patients, they may survive CPR but they won't ever be able to leave the hospital.

5.   Nicholas Christakis, *Death Foretold: Prophecy and Prognosis in Medical Care* (Chicago: University of Chicago Press, 1999), pp. 1–29

6.   A controversial term, the debate over the value-laden concept of "futility" is most publicly focused on the right of individuals to reject treatments, i.e., "do not resuscitate" (DNR) orders relating to the decision whether or not to start CPR. A newer category is DNI, "do not intubate," which is simply another way of refusing mechanical ventilation.

Treatment (SUPPORT) trial failed to change physicians' behaviors or measurable outcomes and suggests limits in physicians' ability to detect end-of-life even when given prognostic statistics. [7] Though most deaths in an ICU are preceded by withholding or withdrawing life-sustaining therapy (LST) through issuing a "stop order," the median predicted chance for two-month survival by attending physicians in the SUPPORT trial was no better than 50–50 just one week before death.[8] Even the eventual decision to "turn off the machines" and the process surrounding that decision varies between ICUs nationally and internationally; there are no standards of practice that say treatment must stop or continue.[9] The hallmark Karen Ann Quinlan decision in 1976 advanced a body of case law that addressed "right-to-die" issues involving principles of autonomy, informed consent and substituted judgment (authorized surrogates). However, within the last 15 years there has been a shift toward the other direction, with people now asking for the very treatments that others fought to reject.[10]

7.   "A Controlled Trial to Improve Care for Seriously Ill Hospitalized Patients: The Study to Understand Prognoses and Preferences for Outcomes and Risks of Treatments (SUPPORT)," *Journal of the American Medical Association* 274.20 (1995), pp. 1591–98. This is the largest study of its kind with 9000 sample patients (each given at least a 50 percent chance of dying within six months) hospitalized in the ICUs of five academic health centers. The SUPPORT investigators designed an intervention to improve hospital care for these seriously ill patients and their families. The results are very controversial and will be discussed.

8.   David Crippen, "Practical Aspects of Life Support Withdrawal: A Critical Care Physician's Ppinion," *Clinical Intensive Care* 2 (1991), pp. 260–65 Stop orders might be time or event related, given when no improvement occurs within a defined period or when respiratory, heart or renal failure occurs.

9.   Jean Carlet *et al.*, "Challenges in End-of-Life Care in the ICU: Statement of the 5th International Consensus Conference in Critical Care, Brussels, Belgium, April 2003," *Intensive Care Medicine* 30.5 (2004), pp. 770–84 The jurors at this conference identified numerous problems with end of life in the ICU including variability in practice, inadequate predictive models for death, elusive knowledge of patient preferences, poor communication between staff and surrogates, insufficient or absent training of health care providers, the use of imprecise and insensitive terminology, and incomplete documentation in the medical records.

10. There have been recent court cases involving surrogates who have refused to allow treatment to stop, for example *Gilgunn v. Massachusetts General Hospital* (1995) in which a daughter fought the decision to allow DNR orders to be placed on her comatose mother's chart. After legal consideration, the hospital's Optimum Care Committee noted that CPR was not a "genuine therapeutic

The expectation of modern critical care evolved into the idea that a high technology care plan including CPR could do miracles. But in reality, that care plan led to another population, one composed mainly of older patients who were left not alive (in the sense of being capable of enjoying life) and not able to die (because technology temporarily arrested the disease process but did not reverse it). And by 2018, more than 70 million Americans over the age of 65 will be facing difficult end-of-life decisions for themselves.

Medical systems are deeply embedded in culture and, as such, structure our experience of disease; the identification and definition of illness depends on both the physician's explanation and patient's personal experience. Given the social context of critical care medicine, this article will attempt to explore the rescue-culture of modern medicine and the role of Advance Care Planning/Directives in giving voice to and respecting a patient's choice in end-of-life care.

Patients Don't Die: They Code[11]

Removal of mechanical ventilation (extubation) is the most common factor preceding ICU deaths; it is also the life-support system that clinicians are most hesitant about removing and requires a patient or surrogate's consent.[12] Informed consent, as it is commonly understood, is a process in which the attending physician suggests a therapy or procedure and the

option" for the critically ill patient. DNR orders were written and the attending began to wean the patient from mechanical ventilation citing "imminent death." The patient died three days later and the daughter subsequently sued for neglect and emotional distress. The jury returned a decision in favor of MGH stating that the care withheld in the patient's case would have been futile because it would not have provided a cure. Alexander Capron, "Abandoning a Waning Life," *Hastings Center Report* 25.4 (1995), pp. 24–26.

11.   This is an often-heard hospital saying.

12.   G. D. Rubenfeld and S. W. Crawford, "Principles and Practice of Withdrawing Life-Sustaining Treatment in the ICU" in J. Randall Curtis and Gordon D. Rubenfeld (eds), *Managing Death in the ICU: The Transition from Cure to Comfort* (London: Oxford University Press, 2000), pp. 134–41. MV termination is likely to lead to profound discomfort due to dyspnea; since withdrawal poses the greatest problems with ensuring comfort, all other life-support devices are normally withdrawn before the ventilator. While protocols have been made for diagnosing brain death, there has been no such protocol, either nationally or internationally, for diagnosing PVS. EEG's are of limited usefulness in that the findings are unspecific, i.e., some diffuse activity along different brain-wave bandwidths exist.

patient (or healthcare agent/proxy) consents. There are different interpretations of what this really means: in the most literal sense, it means signing forms required for certain invasive procedures (while other procedures do not); a less literal interpretation means any additional therapies or changes in plan of care must be communicated and understood by the patient or healthcare proxy. The one instance where mechanical ventilation and other life-saving therapy such as hydration or dialysis may be legally terminated without notification or informed consent is in the case of brain death.[13]

Decisions to discontinue life-sustaining therapy in patients in persistent vegetative states (PVS) are fundamentally an application of "medical futility." However, although the argument for cessation of treatment is one that many find compelling, this decision often hinges on advance directives or other clear evidence of the patient's wishes. In the case of Mrs D, her surgery mandated she be a full code. Individual autonomy and patient interests, as noted earlier, are most readily seen in Do Not Resuscitate/Do Not Intubate (DNR/DNI) orders.

In 1983, the President's Commission for the Study of Ethical Problems in Medicine recommended that hospitals adopt DNR/DNI procedures to ensure that patients or their surrogates participate in decision-making about such orders. This emphasis on decision-making and personal autonomy grows directly out of our culture's strong emphasis on individualism and personal autonomy; this focus soon translated into a strong interest in advanced directives in the form of living wills and healthcare proxies. The Patient Self-Determination Act of 1991 required that all healthcare institutions receiving Medicare or Medicaid inform patients of their right under state law to execute advance directives.[14] However, the SUPPORT study suggests that the law's impact is largely ceremonial – influencing how physicians document their decisions on DNR orders *not* the processes through which such decisions are made.[15]

13. Four factors of the so-called Harvard Criteria for determining brain death have been widely recognized and accepted in clinical practice in the United States; unreceptivity and unresponsivity, no spontaneous movements or breathing, no reflexes and the absence of elicitable reflexes, and flat EEG's taken twice within at least a 24–hour period. Gary S. Belkin, "Brain Death and the Historical Understanding of Bioethics," *Journal of the History of Medicine and Allied Sciences* 58.3 (July 2003), pp. 325–61. Europeans do not have the EEG requirement. The Ad Hoc Committee of the Harvard Medical School to Examine the Definition of Brain Death was formed in 1968.

14. Elizabeth Leibold McCloskey, "The Patient Self-Determination Act," *Kennedy Institute of Ethics Journal* 1 (1991), pp. 163–69.

15. Designed as a randomized controlled trial (RCT), SUPPORT patients and

Although 31 percent of the patients expressed a preference not to be resuscitated, slightly fewer than half of their physicians did not respect or know about the patient's advance directives. DNR orders were written very late, in the majority of the cases only 24 hours before death. And, most sobering, 40 percent of the patients had severe and potentially treatable pain for more than several days before dying. Adoption of DNR orders does not ensure patients or their surrogates participation in the decision-making concerning *when* to institute such orders; most patients and families are still left in the dark as to how the decision to withdraw life-sustaining therapy in the ICU is made. Once DNR orders are written, the person most influenced is the attending physician.

The SUPPORT trial showed no benefit associated in using trained study nurses to provide prognostic data to patients, families, and physicians, or identifying patient preferences for end-of-life care, providing this information to physicians, and in facilitating communication between patients, families, and clinicians.[16] There have been a number of suggestions as to why the SUPPORT intervention did not result in better end-of-life care, but methodologically, running a behavior-change intervention along a strictly biomedical model of inquiry without consideration of human motivation is faulty. The leading hypothesis is that the intervention did not work because it simply did not influence the systems of care at the target institutions; the physicians in charge.[17]

their physicians were randomized by physician specialty group to receive intervention or usual medical care. The intervention consisted of three components: nurses were trained to hold advance planning conversations about the use of LST, doctors were provided with reports summarizing patient's treatment preferences and desires for information, and a computer generated report of survival probability concerning life expectancy and CPR survivability was available to all staff. During Phase I, baseline data was collected on a broad range of patient interests, including DNR orders and comfort-only measures. Phase II showed no impact of the intervention in the experimental sites on any of the designated outcome measures which were timing of DNR orders, physician-patient agreement on DNR orders, number of desirable days in ICU, pain, and the amount of health care consumed.

16.   Critical care nurses in particular expressed frustration with the end-of-life care provided by physicians and demonstrated much higher levels of dissatisfaction than physicians with the end-of-life care in the ICU. Naomi Hodde *et al.*, "Factors Associated with Nurse Assessment of the Quality of Dying and Death in the Intensive Care Unit", *Critical Care Medicine* 32.8 (2004), pp. 1648–53.

17.   Another critique is conceptual: the intervention placed too much hope in advance directives as a means for improving end-of-life care, with emphasis on individualism and personalized decision over a family's love, support and care.

"The Pursuit of Disease or the Care of the Sick?"[18]

So where does that leave the person involved in a devastating accident, who has never told family or friends what their wishes might be if they could not speak for themselves? The framing of the SUPPORT intervention was built on an overly rationalistic and individualistic concept of healthcare, one that is not shared by all segments of our decidedly pluralistic society. It is very rare for all parties involved in making end-of-life decisions for a family member like Mrs D to come to consensus without a clear directive as to what her explicit wishes are.

In my work as a hospital chaplain, I'm often involved with patients and families as they go through the process of choosing and implementing a legally binding advance care directive. There are two forms of advance directives: a Living Will and a Medical Power of Attorney (Health Care Proxy). A Living Will is a document that specifies what type of medical treatments, including life-sustaining interventions, you would or would not want if you were unable to communicate (feeding tube, ventilation support, and so on). A Health Care Proxy (HCP) is a document that appoints some-one to make medical decisions for you if you are in a situation where you can't make them yourself: that person serves as your Health Care Agent.

The laws governing advance directives vary from state to state and are easily accessible by contacting a local hospital or town hall.[19] Most states have a preference for which directive to use; for example, in Massachusetts a Health Care Proxy is the preferred directive. The Proxy is a simple form that comes with instructions, is free of charge to prepare and requires no lawyer but does require the signature of two witnesses. Legally binding in Mas-sachusetts, the Proxy can be canceled or changed at any time and replaced with a new one. Living Wills are not legally binding in MA but are helpful in determining a person's wishes, especially if there is conflict with the per-son's Health Care Agent.

Over the last decade, there has been a nation-wide effort to support Advance Care Planning in making your choices known about the medical treatment you would want if an illness or injury suddenly left you unable to make or communicate healthcare choices. However, as of 2012, 56 percent of Americans had not communicated their end-of-life preferences with others.[20]

18. Eric Cassell, *The Nature of Suffering and the Goals of Medicine* (Oxford: Oxford University Press, 2004). This is the title of Ch. 7.

19. There are differences in the legal status of living wills in each state: in New York a living will is actually not a legal document and medical decisions may not be based on it alone.

20. Survey of Californians by the California HealthCare Foundation (2012) – see

Advance Care Planning is important for a number of reasons:

- Guides those who care about you in a difficult time
- Gives you the chance to fully understand the benefits and risks of treatment options
- Makes your choices known
- Plans for the unexpected

Most people simply put in the names of family members as their Health Care Agents; very few patients ever have in-depth conversations with the people named in the Proxy, and many feel uncomfortable having such conversations from a hospital bed. This can lead to disastrous results like that of Mrs D; most cases brought to hospital end-of-life ethics committees involve making a decision for a patient when their preferences are not known or who have no Health Care Proxy.

Perhaps the easiest way to begin the process is by remembering past experiences: have you or other people you know faced difficult medical decisions during times of a serious illness or accident? (Think of the Terri Schiavo case.) What did you learn from these past experiences? What kind of situation would be unacceptable to you? What do you value most about your life? Next, consider what medical choices you may face in the future, especially if you have a diagnosed medical condition that might lead to a serious hospitalization. Talk to your clinicians to understand the medical choices you might face. For example, what if you couldn't communicate with your family and the choice had to be made to insert a feeding or breathing tube; what would you want them to do?

The next step is to actually choose your Health Care Agent(s); they do not have to be a family member, but they must be over 18 and willing and able to accept the role. [21] This means they are able to make decisions at stressful times and should be available to talk with your healthcare providers as needed (which should preclude the uncle living 3,000 miles away). The

more at The Conversation Project: http://theconversationproject.org/#sthash.nWJB4SEu.dpuf.

21.   For many family members, the wish that a loved one be allowed to die is followed by guilt; sometimes family members act out their guilt over harboring such secret desires by vigorously opposing any suggestion that treatment be limited. "In both the Dostoevsky novel (*The Brothers Karamazov*) and the ICU, a strange pattern of communication emerges by which people do not forthrightly express their wishes." Martha M. Montello and John D. Lantos, "The Karamazov Complex: Dostoevsky and DNR Orders," *Perspectives in Biology and Medicine* 45.2 (2002), pp. 190–99.

Health Care Agent only acts if you are unable to communicate your wishes, for example, if you are unconscious or in a coma or state of delirium. It is important for you and your Agent to take the time to have an in-depth conversation; does he/she know you well enough to know what gives your life meaning? If not, is he/she willing to spend time talking with you to find out? Does he/she know your choices for medical treatments in different situations? He/she may decide whether to start, continue, or stop treatments that may include making life and death choices.

Many people use the legal document "Five Wishes" which combines both a Living Will and Health Care Proxy and are available at most hospitals/clinics. Accepted in all but eight states, it poses questions and guidelines that promote conversation and understanding of a person's wishes concerning end-of-life care. However, none of this matters if the information is not shared with others; it is most important to give copies of your Health Care Proxy or Advance Care Directive to everyone involved in your healthcare: family, doctor, lawyer, and so on.

As seen by the results of the SUPPORT study, patients and/or families need to be proactive in advocating adherence to their Advance Care Directive to any and all clinicians involved in their medical treatment plan. *Keep the conversation going*…the more others know your wishes concerning end-of-life care, the better chance you have at having someone listen. The time, for humanists and all others, to act is now.

Advance Directive Websites

Five Wishes Advance Directive Booklet (Aging with Dignity)	http://www.agingwithdignity.org
American Association of Retired Persons (AARP): Beginning the Conversation about the End of Life	http://www.aarp.org/relationships/caregiving-resource-center/info-08–2010/elc_beginning_the_conversation_about_end_of_life.html
Compassion and Choices	http://community.compassionandchoices.org/sslpage.aspx?pid=484&nccsm=15&__nccscid=14&__nccsct=Advance+Directives
American Bar Association: Tool Kit for Healthcare Advance Planning	http://www.americanbar.org/groups/law_aging/resources/consumer_s_toolkit_for_health_care_advance_planning.html
American Hospital Association: Put It In Writing	http://www.putitinwriting.org/putitinwriting_app/index.jsp
Caring Connections: Advance Care Plan.	http://caringinfo.org/i4a/pages/index.cfm?pageid=3284
National Healthcare Decisions Day	http://www.nhdd.org/

Bibliography

"A Controlled Trial to Improve Care for Seriously Ill Hospitalized Patients: The Study to Understand Prognoses and Preferences for Outcomes and Risks of Treatments (SUPPORT)." *The Journal of the American Medical Association* 274.20 (November 22, 1995), pp. 1591–98.

Abrahamson, Brant, and Fred Smith. *Thinking Logically: A Study of Common Fallacies.* Tuscon, AZ: GP, 1993.

Adler, Felix. *Life and Destiny.* New York: McClure, Phillips, and Co., 1913.

—*An Ethical Philosophy of Life.* New York: D. Appleton-Century Co., 1918.

"American Atheists, Inc." *Facebook*, March 9, 2012.

American Humanist Association. "Humanist Manifestoes I (1933), II (1973), and III (2003)." Accessed December 2, 2013. http://americanhumanist.org.

"An Open Letter to Humanists: Donating to Humanist Charities," n.d. http://americanhumanist.org/HNN/details/2011-09-an-open-letter.

Angus, Derek, A.E. Barnato, W.T. Linde-Zwirble, L.A. Weissfeld, R.S. Watson, T. Rickert, G.D. Rubenfeld, "Use of Intensive Care at the End of Life in the United States: An Eoidemiologic Study." *Critical Care Medicine* 32 (2004).

Bass, Ellen. *Mules of Love.* Rochester, New York: BOA Editions, 2002.

Batchelor, Stephen. *Buddhism without Beliefs.* New York: Riverhead Trade, 1998.

Beauvoir, Simone de. *The Second Sex.* Random House, 1949.

Belkin, Gary S. "Brain Death and the Historical Understanding of Bioethics." *Journal of the History of Medicine and Allied Sciences* 58.3 (July 2003), pp. 325–61.

Bhaerman, Bob, ed. *Establishing Humanist Education Programs for Children.* Kochhar Humanist Education Center, 2011, http://www.americanhumanist.org/system/storage/63/d4/4/2129/childrens_manual_web.pdf.

Black, Algernon. "Three Wishes at Death." In Black, *Without Burnt Offerings: Ceremonies of Humanism.* New York: The Viking Press, 1974.

British Humanist Association. "Good Causes and Charities." n.d. https://humanism.org.uk/humanism/humanism-today/humanists-doing/good-causes-and-charities/.

California HealthCare Foundation. "The Conversation Project," (2012), http://theconversationproject.org/.

Camus, Albert. *The Myth of Sisyphus and Other Essays.* New York: Vintage International, 1991.

—*The Rebel: An Essay on Man in Revolt.* New York: Vintage International, 1991.

Capron, Alexander Morgan. "Abandoning a Waning Life." *Hastings Center Report* 25.4 (1995), pp. 24–26.

Carey, Benedict. "This is your Life (and How You Tell It)." *The New York Times*, May 22, 2007, sec. Health / Mental Health & Behavior. http://www.nytimes.com/2007/05/22/health/psychology/22narr.html.

Carlet, Jean, Lambertus G. Thijs, Massimo Antonelli, Joan Cassell, Peter Cox,

Nicholas Hill, Charles Hinds, Jorge Manuel Pimentel, Konrad Reinhart, and Boyd Taylor Thompson. "Challenges in End-of-Life Care in the ICU. Statement of the 5th International Consensus Conference in Critical Care: Brussels, Belgium, April 2003." *Intensive Care Medicine* 30.5 (2004), pp. 770–84.

Cassell, Eric J. *The Nature of Suffering and the Goals of Medicine*. Oxford: Oxford University Press, 2004.

"Changing Minds: Behind the Rise in Support for Gay Marriage." *Pew Research Center for the People and the Press*, March 21, 2013. http://www.people-press.org/2013/03/21/gay-marriage-changing-opinions/.

"Children Who Lose a Parent to Suicide More Likely to Die the Same Way, Study Finds." *Science Daily*, April 21, 2010.

Christakis, Nicholas A. *Death Foretold: Prophecy and Prognosis in Medical Care*. University of Chicago Press, 1999.

Cimino, Richard, and Christopher Smith. "The New Atheism and the Formation of the Imagined Secularist Community." *Journal of Media and Religion* 10.1 (2011), pp. 24–38.

Copson, Andrew. "Face to Faith." *The Guardian*, October 30, 2009, sec. Comment is free. http://www.theguardian.com/commentisfree/belief/2009/oct/30/john-stuart-mill-on-liberty.

Crippen, David. "Practical Aspects of Life Support Withdrawal: A Critical Care Physician's Opinion." *Clinical Intensive Care* 2 (1991), pp. 260–65.

Darwin, Charles. *The Descent of Man*. London: John Murray, 1871.

Dawkins, Richard. "Genesmanship." In *The Selfish Gene*. Oxford University Press, 1989.

De Botton, Alain. *Religion for Atheists: A Non-Believer's Guide to the Uses of Religion*. New York: Vintage, 2013.

Descola, Philippe. *Par-delà nature et culture*. Paris: Gallimard, 2005.

Diem, Susan J., John D. Lantos, and James A. Tulsky. "Cardiopulmonary Resuscitation on Television – Miracles and Misinformation." *New England Journal of Medicine* 334.24 (1996), pp. 1578–82.

Dobrin, Arthur. *Love your Neighbor: Stories of Values and Virtues*. New York: Scholastic, 2000.

—*Teaching Right from Wrong: 40 Things You Can Do to Raise a Moral Child*. New York: Berkley Trade, 2001.

—"Religious Ethics: A Source Book." http://arthurdobrin.files.wordpress.com/2008/08/religious-ethics.pdf.

Dostoevsky, Fyodor. *The Brothers Karamazov*. Grigoriy, 2014.

Ehrman, Bart. "Biblical Scholarship and the Right to Know." *The Humanist* (November/December 2011). http://thehumanist.org/november-december-2011/biblical-scholarship-and-the-right-to-know/

Elder, Linda. *Critical Thinking for Children*. Tomales, CA: Foundation for Critical Thinking, 2006.

Evans, Robert. "U.N. Told Atheists Face Discrimination around Globe." *Reuters*. February 25, 2013. http://www.reuters.com/article/2013/02/25/us-rights-atheists-idUSBRE91O0Z920130225.

Fromm, Erich. *Escape from Freedom*. New York: Holt, Rinehart & Winston, 1941.

—*The Art of Loving*. New York: Harper & Row, 1956.

Ganz, Marshall. "Why Stories Matter," March 2009. http://sojo.net/magazine/2009/03/why-stories-matter.

Ghosh, Bobby. "Mosque Controversy: Does America Have a Muslim Problem?" *Time*, August 30, 2010. http://www.time.com.

Gilding, Paul. *The Great Disruption: How the Climate Crisis Will Transform the Global Economy.* Bloomsbury, 2011.

Ginges, Jeremy, Ian Hansen, and Ara Norenzayan. "Religion and Support for Suicide Attacks." *Psychological Science* 20.2 (February 1, 2009), pp. 224–30.

"Global Footprint Network: HOME - Ecological Footprint - Ecological Sustainability." n.d. http://www.footprintnetwork.org/.

Golden, Caitlin. "Beyond Interfaith: Why We Changed our Name." *NonProphet Status*, July 14, 2011. http://nonprophetstatus.com/2011/07/14/beyond-interfaith-why-we-changed-our-name/.

Goodman, David C., Elliott S. Fisher, John E. Wennberg, Jonathan S. Skinner, Scott Chasan-Taber, and Kristen K. Bronner. "Tracking Improvement in the Care of Chronically Ill Patients: Dartmouth Atlas Brief." *The Dartmouth Institute for Health Policy & Clinical Practice* (June 12, 2013).

Grayling, A. C. "Hope." In *Meditations for the Humanist: Ethics for a Secular Age.* Oxford: Oxford University Press, 2002.

Hawken, Paul. *Blessed Unrest: How the Largest Movement in the World Came into Being, and Why No One Saw It Coming.* New York: Viking Penguin, 2007.

Hecht, Jennifer Michael. *Stay: A History of Suicide and the Philosophies against It.* New Haven: Yale University Press, 2013.

Hitchens, Christopher, and Tony Blair. *Hitchens vs. Blair: Be It Resolved Religion is a Force for Good in the World.* Toronto: House of Anansi, 2011.

Hodde, Naomi M., Ruth A. Engelberg, Patsy D. Treece, Kenneth P. Steinberg, and J. Randall Curtis. "Factors Associated with Nurse Assessment of the Quality of Dying and Death in the Intensive Care Unit." *Critical Care Medicine* 32.8 (August 2004), pp. 1648–53.

"Human Development Index (HDI)." n.d. http://hdr.undp.org/en.

"Humanist Manifesto I." American Humanist Association. http://americanhumanist.org/Humanism/Humanist_Manifesto_I.

"Humanist Manifesto II." American Humanist Association. http://americanhumanist.org/Humanism/Humanist_Manifesto_II.

"Humanist Manifesto III." American Humanist Association. http://americanhumanist.org/Humanism/Humanist_Manifesto_III.

IFYC. *The Interfaith Leader's Toolkit.* Chicago: IFYC, 2009.

"In God's Name? Evaluating the Links between Religious Extremism and Terrorism." *Pew Research Center's Religion & Public Life Project*, October 21, 2005. http://www.pewforum.org/2005/10/21/in-gods-name-evaluating-the-links-between-religious-extremism-and-terrorism/.

"Journey of the Universe." n.d. http://www.journeyoftheuniverse.org/.

Klug, Francesca. *Values for a Godless Age: The Story of the UK's New Bill of Rights.* London: Penguin, 2000.

Kramer, Stephen P. *How to Think like a Scientist: Answering Questions by the Scientific Method.* New York: HarperCollins, 1987.

Lahti, David. "Why Does Religion Keep Telling Us We're Bad?" *The Guardian*, November 22, 2011. http://www.theguardian.com/commentisfree/belief/2011/nov/22/religion-bad-evolution-religious-admonitions.

Lamont, Corliss. *The Philosophy of Humanism.* New York: Continuum, 1990.

Lewis, Barbara A., *The Kid's Guide to Service Projects: Over 500 Service Ideas for Young People Who Want to Make a Difference*. Minneapolis: Free Spirit Publishing, 1995.

—*The Kid's Guide to Social Action: How to Solve the Social Problems You Choose – and Turn Creative Thinking into Positive Action*. Minneapolis: Free Spirit Publishing, 1998.

Levy, Mitchell M. "Dying in America." *Critical Care Medicine* 32.3 (March 2004), pp. 879–80.

Lincoln, Abraham. *Speeches and Letters of Abraham Lincoln, 1832-1865*, n.d.

Lupton, Robert D. *Toxic Charity: How the Church Hurts Those They Help (and How to Reverse It)*. New York: HarperOne, 2011.

Lymari, Morales. "Knowing Someone Gay/Lesbian Affects Views of Gay Issues," May 29, 2009. http://www.gallup.com/poll/118931/knowing-someone-gay-lesbian-affects-views-gay-issues.aspx.

Manier, Bénédicte. *Un million de mévolutions tranquilles. Travail/argent/habitat/santé/environment. Comment les citoyens changent le monde*. Paris: les Liens qui libèrent, 2012.

McCloskey, Elizabeth Leibold. "The Patient Self-Determination Act." *Kennedy Institute of Ethics Journal* 1.2 (1991), pp. 163–69.

McCreight, Jen. "Atheism+." *Blag Hag Blog*, August 19, 2012. http://freethought-blogs.com.

McGowan, Dale. *Parenting Beyond Belief: On Raising Ethical, Caring Kids without Religion*. New York: AMACOM, 2007.

McGowan, Dale, Molleen Matsumura, Amanda Metskas and Jan Devor. *Raising Freethinkers: A Practical Guide for Parenting Beyond Belief*. New York: AMACOM, 2009.

Mill, John Stuart. *On Liberty*. London: Longman, Roberts & Green Co., 1869.

—*The Subjection of Women*. London: Longmans, Green, Readers & Dryer, 1869.

Montello, Martha M., and John D. Lantos. "The Karamazov Complex: Dostoevsky and DNR Orders." *Perspectives in Biology and Medicine* 45.2 (2002), pp. 190–99.

Morain, Lloyd and Mary. *Humanism as the Nest Step*. Washington, DC: Humanist Press, 2008.

Morin, Edgar, and Anne Brigitte Kern. *Homeland Earth: A Manifesto for the New Millennium*. Hampton Press, 1999.

Myers, PZ. "What is This 'Interfaith' Nonsense, Anyway?" *Pharyngula*, March 19, 2011. http://scienceblogs.com/pharyngula/2011/03/19/what-is-this-interfaith-nonsen/.

"NASPA | Student Affairs Administrators in Higher Education." *NASPA*, n.d. http://www.naspa.org/.

National Leaders Council. "Life Passage Ceremonies." New York: American Ethical Union, 2002.

"'Nones' on the Rise: Religion and the Unaffiliated," October 9, 2012. http://www.pewforum.org/2012/10/09/nones-on-the-rise-religion/.

Norman, Richard, ed. *The Case for Secularism: A Neutral State in an Open Society*. London: British Humanist Association, 2007.

Nussbaum, Martha C. *Political Emotions: Why Love matters for Justice*. Cambridge, MA: The Belknap Press of Harvard University, 2013.

Pape, Robert. *Dying to Win: The Strategic Logic of Suicide Terrorism*. New York: Random House, 2006.

Patel, Eboo. *Acts of Faith: The Story of an American Muslim, in the Struggle for the Soul of a Generation*. Boston: Beacon Press, 2007.

—"Religion Today: Bomb, Barrier or Bridge?" *The Huffington Post*, August 5, 2010. http://www.huffingtonpost.com/eboo-patel/religion-today-bomb-barri_b_667817.html.

Patel, Eboo, and Cassie Meyer. "Defining Religious Pluarlism: A Response to Robert McKim." *Journal of Collee and Character* 11.2 (2010), pp. 1–4.

Paul, Richard, and Linda Elder. *The Miniature Guide to Critical Thinking: Concepts and Tools.* www.criticalthinking.org.

Pinker, Steven. *How the Mind Works*. New York: W. W. Norton, 1999.

Pinn, Anthony B. *By These Hands: A Documentary History of African American Humanism.* New York: New York University Press, 2001.

—*African American Humanist Principles: Living and Thinking like the Children of Nimrod.* New York: Palgrave Macmillan, 2004.

—*The End of God-Talk: An African American Humanist Theology*. New York: Oxford University Press, 2012.

Popper, Karl Raimund, Václav Havel, and Ernst Hans Josef Gombrich. *The Open Society and its Enemies*. New York: Routledge, 1945.

"Public Remains Conflicted Over Islam." *Pew Research Center for the People and the Press*, August 24, 2010. http://www.people-press.org/2010/08/24/public-remains-conflicted-over-islam/.

Putnam, Robert D. "E Pluribus Unum: Diversity and Community in the Twenty-First Century." *Scandinavian Political Studies* 30.2. The 2006 Johan Skytte Prize Lectures (June 15, 2007). http://onlinelibrary.wiley.com/doi/10.1111/j.1467-9477.2007.00176.x/full.

Radest, Howard. *Toward Common Ground.* New York: Unger, 1969.

Raskin, Paul, Global Scenario Group, *et al. Great Transition: The Promise and Lure of the Times Ahead*. Stockholm: Stockholm Environment Institute, 2002.

Reiser, Oliver L. *The Promise of Scientific Humanism.* New York: Oskar Piest, 1940. http://americanhumanist.org/what_we_do/publications/Humanism_as_the_Next_Step/Chapter_7:_Applying_Humanism_to_Social_Problems.

"Religion among the Millennials." *Pew Research Center's Religion & Public Life Project*, February 17, 2010. http://www.pewforum.org/2010/02/17/religion-among-the-millennials/.

"Religious Landscape Survey." *Pew Research Center's Religion & Public Life Project*. http://religions.pewforum.org/

Rubenfeld, G. D., and S. W. Crawford. "Principles and Practice of Withdrawing Life-Sustaining Treatment in the ICU." In J. Randall Curtis and Gordon D. Rubenfeld, eds, *Managing Death in the ICU : The Transition from Cure to Comfort*, pp. 134–41. London: Oxford University Press, 2000.

Russell, Bertrand. *Why I Am Not a Christian and Other Essays on Religion and Related Subjects*. New York: Touchstone, 1967.

Sagan, Carl. *Cosmos.* New York: Random House, 1980.

Saslow, Laura R., Robb Willer, Matthew Feinberg, Paul K. Piff, Katharine Clark, Dacher Keltner, and Sarina R. Saturn. "My Brother's Keeper? Compassion Predicts Generosity More among Less Religious Individuals." *Social Psychological and Personality Science*, April 26, 2012. http://spp.sagepub.com/content/early/2012/04/25/1948550612444137

Sartre, Jean-Paul. "Existentialism is a Humanism." In *Existentialism from Dostoevsky to Sartre*, ed. Walter Arnold Kaufmann. New York: Meridian, 1989.

Schaeffer, Jean-Marie. *La fin de l'exception humaine*. Paris: Gallimard, 2007.

Schafersman, Steven. "Critical Thinking and its Relation to Science and Humanism." 1998. www.freeinquiry.com.

Scott, Eugenie, and Glenn Branch. *Not in our Classrooms: Why Intelligent Design is Wrong for our Schools.* Boston: Beacon Press, 2006.

Sen, Amartya. *The Argumentative Indian.* New York: Picador, 2005.

—*Identity and Violence.* New York: W. W. Norton, 2006.

Seneca, Lucius Annaeus. *Letters to Lucilius*. Oxford: Clarendon, 1932.

Shariff, Azim F., and Ara Norenzayan. "God Is Watching You: Priming God Concepts Increases Prosocial Behavior in an Anonymous Economic Game." *Psychological Science* 18.9 (2007), pp. 809–809.

Spetter, Matthew Ies. *Man the Reluctant Brother.* New York: The Fieldston Press, 1967.

Stangroom, Jeremy. "Atheists, Morality and Distant Others." *Talking Philosophy*, August 19, 2012. http://blog.talkingphilosophy.com/?p=5625.

Stedman, Chris. *Faitheist: How an Atheist Found Common Ground with the Religious*. Beacon Press, 2012.

"Tamil Tigers: Suicide Bombing Innovators." *NPR.org*, May 21, 2009. http://www.npr.org/templates/story/story.php?storyId=104391493.

"The Earth Charter." http://www.earthcharterinaction.org/content/pages/Read-the-Charter.html.

"The President's Interfaith and Community Service Campus Challenge," http://www.whitehouse.gov/administration/eop/ofbnp/interfaithservice.

"The Universal Declaration of Human Rights," December 10, 1948. http://www.un.org/en/documents/udhr/.

Thoreau, Henry David. *Walden*. Princeton: Princeton University Press, 1973.

Thucydides. *The History of the Peloponnesian War*. Vol. 2. Edward Earle, 1818.

Tucker, Mary Evelyn, and John Grim, eds. *The Religions of the World and Ecology Book Series*. Yale: Yale University Press, 1997–2004. http://fore.research.yale.edu/publications/books/ cswr/.

Varshney, Ashutosh. *Ethnic Conflict and Civic Life: Hindus and Muslims in India.* New York: Yale University Press, 2003.

Vidal, John. "China and India 'Water Grab' Dams Put Ecology of Himalayas in Danger." *The Guardian*, August 10, 2013, sec. Global development. http://www.theguardian.com/global-development/2013/aug/10/china-india-water-grab-dams-himalayas-danger.

Walker, Alice. *Living by the Word*. New York: Harcourt Brace Jovanovich, 1988.

Weiming, Tu. "The Continuity of Being: Chinese Visions of Nature." In *Confucianism and Ecology*, ed. Mary Evelyn Tucker and John Berthrong. Cambridge, MA: Harvard University Press, 1998.

—"Beyond the Enlightenment Mentality." In *Confucianism and Ecology*, ed. Mary Evelyn Tucker and John Berthrong. Cambridge, MA: Harvard University Press, 1998.

—"The Ecological Turn in New Confucian Humanism." In *Confucian Spirituality: Volume 2*, ed. Mary Evelyn Tucker and Tu Weiming. New York: Crossroad, 2004.

Whedon, Joss. "The True Enemy of Humanism." See Mockingbird April 15, 2009. www.mbird.com/2009/04/joss-whedon-on-humanism-and-its-enemy/

Wilcox, Holly C., Paul Kuramoto, Niklas Langstrom Lichtenstein, David A. Brent, and Bo Runeson. "Psychiatric Morbidity, Violent Crime, and Suicide among Children and Adolescents Exposed to Parental Death." *Journal of the American Academy of Child & Adolescent Psychiatry* 49.5 (May 2010), pp. 514–23.

Wilkinson, Richard, and Kate Pickett. *The Spirit Level: Why Equality is Better for Everyone*. Penguin Books, 2010.

Williams, Jessica. "Faith, Hope and Charity," *New Humanist* (May 31, 2007). http://rationalist.org.uk/articles/941/faith-hope-and-charity.

Williams, Margery. *The Velveteen Rabbit (or How Toys Become Real)*. New York: George H. Doran, 1922.

Wine, Sherwin. *Judaism Beyond God.* New York: Society for Humanistic Judaism, 1985.

Sherwin Wine, "Reflections," in *A Life of Courage.* New York: International Institute for Secular Humanistic Judaism, 2004.

Wintermute, Carol. "The Aesthetic Pillar of Humanism." *Humanism Today* 13 (1999). http://www.humanismtoday.org/vol13/wintermute.html.

—"A Vision of Humanist Education for our Complex World." *Essays in the Philosophy of Humanism* 18.1 (Spring-Summer, 2010), pp. 71-80.

Wittgenstein, Ludwig. *Notebooks*. Chicago: University of Chicago Press, 1984.

Wolfelt, Alan D. Creating Meaningful Funeral Ceremonies: A Guide for Caregivers. Fort Collins, CO: Companion Press, 1994.

Wollstonecraft, Mary. *A Vindication of the Rights of Women*. Boston: Peter Edes, 1792.

Wright, Richard. *Black Boy.* New York: Harper & Row, 1966.

Zak, Paul J. *The Moral Molecule: The Source of Love and Prosperity.* New York: Dutton, 2012.

US Bureau of Justice Statistics, n.d. http://www.bjs.gov/content/glance/viort.cfm.

www.criticalthinking.org/

www.criticalthinking.org/about/internationalCenter.shtml

www.freeinquiry.com

www.freeinquiry.com/critical-thinking.html

www.philosopher.org/

Index

CPSIA information can be obtained at www.ICGtesting.com
Printed in the USA
BVOW08s0848190115

383625BV00001B/3/P